WORKBOOK

Anna Richardson

CONTENTS

3

1A

Vocabulary
Countries

1 Put the letters in the correct order to make countries.

1 aCaadn   _Canada_
2 oMxice   ....
3 ailnahTd   ....
4 ndaloP   ....
5 naetgnAir   ....
6 apnSi   ....

2 Write the country for each flag.

1 _the UK_

2 ....

3 ....

4 ....

5 ....

6 ....

7 ....

8 ....

3 Complete the sentences with countries from Exercises 1 and 2.

1 Are you from S_pain_   ?
2 I'm from A.................... .
3 You're from M.................... .
4 Are you from P.................... ?
5 I'm not from C.................... .
6 You aren't from J.................... .

Grammar
be: *I* and *you*

4 Put the words in the correct order to make sentences or questions.

1 you / John / Are / ?
    Are you John?
2 Türkiye / I'm / from .
    ....
3 late / You / aren't .
    ....
4 from / Where / you / are / ?
    ....
5 not / teacher / I'm / a .
    ....
6 on / Am / time / I / ?
    ....
7 Canada / you / Are / from / ?
    ....
8 not / I'm / from / UK / the .
    ....

5 Correct the conversations.

1 Where ~~is~~ you from Inés?
    Where **are** you from Inés?
    I'm from Mexico.
2 **A:** Are you a student?
    B: No, I not.
    ....
3 **A:** Am I late?
    B: No, you not.
    ....
4 **A:** Are you Mehmet?
    B: Yes, I are.
    ....
5 **A:** Am you from Türkiye?
    B: No, I'm not.
    ....
6 **A:** Are you from the US?
    B: Yes, I'm.
    ....
7 **A:** Where are you from?
    B: I from Spain.
    ....
8 **A:** You are a teacher?
    B: No, I'm a student.
    ....

6 Complete the answers with the correct form of *be*. Use short forms.

1 Are you from Poland?   Yes, _I am_ .
2 Are you a doctor?   No, ...
3 Am I late?   No, ...
4 Are you the teacher?   Yes, ...
5 Am I on time?   No, ...
6 Are you from Spain?   Yes, ...

Vocabulary

Jobs

1 Complete the names of the jobs.

1 d o c t o r
2 t _ _ i d _ _ v _ r
3 p _ l _ t
4 s _ _ ool te _ _ he _
5 n _ rs _
6 f _ _ t _ a _ l p _ _ y _ r
7 o _ _ ic _ w _ rk _ _
8 f _ _ m _ r

2 Find eight jobs in the word search. Words are across and down.

C	O	R	S	R	F	A	S	S	C	D	U	P	W
B	O	F	A	N	G	D	O	C	T	O	R	C	L
O	S	J	V	D	A	O	L	H	I	F	A	R	M
L	N	H	X	J	N	U	S	O	F	F	I	D	E
Q	U	P	K	D	E	M	G	O	O	I	L	S	T
Z	R	P	B	O	X	E	Y	L	T	C	E	L	A
H	S	F	L	F	K	E	R	T	B	E	L	Y	X
N	E	M	O	O	W	D	E	E	L	W	Y	R	I
G	L	P	I	L	O	T	L	A	P	O	S	F	D
S	C	K	E	R	R	D	A	C	O	R	N	N	R
S	D	F	A	R	M	E	R	H	I	K	D	X	I
M	A	N	G	C	R	T	A	E	O	E	L	L	V
I	B	S	L	K	Z	T	A	R	P	R	W	B	E
F	O	O	T	B	A	L	L	P	L	A	Y	E	R

3 Write the jobs.

1 _____

2 _____

3 _____

4 _____

5 _____

6 _____

Grammar

be: *he/she/it*

4 Correct the sentences.

1 David isn't from Mexico, ~~it's~~ from Spain.
   *David isn't from Mexico, **he's** from Spain.*

2 Sarah are a teacher.
   ....

3 He is a doctor?
   ....

4 **A:** Is Pablo a pilot?   **B:** No, he aren't.
   ....

5 Where Isabel is from?
   ....

6 She aren't a farmer.
   ....

7 **A:** Is Peter from the US?   **B:** Yes, he are.
   ....

8 It are a small hospital.
   ....

5 Rewrite the sentences using short forms.

1 Kate is from the UK.
   Kate's from the UK.

2 John is not a doctor.
   ....

3 It is not a small office.
   ....

4 Where is James from?
   ....

5 It is a small school.
   ....

6 He is a taxi driver.
   ....

6 Write sentences or questions with the correct form of *be*. Use short forms.

1 he / not / a teacher.
   He isn't a teacher.

2 she / from / Italy?
   ....

3 it / a small hospital?
   ....

4 she / from / Poland.
   ....

5 it / not / a small school.
   ....

6 she / not / a pilot
   ....

7 he / a nurse.
   ....

8 where / she / from?
   ....

Vocabulary

Nationalities

1 Complete the table with countries and nationalities.

Countries	Nationalities
Canada	Canadian
Spain	
	Turkish
Mexico	
	American
Poland	
Japan	
	British
Argentina	
	Thai
Brazil	
	Italian

2 Choose the correct alternatives.

1 He's from <u>the US</u> / *American*.
2 We aren't *Polish* / *Poland*.
3 They aren't *Mexico* / *Mexican*.
4 Are they from *Brazilian* / *Brazil*?
5 He's from *Canadian* / *Canada*.
6 We're *Italian* / *Italy*.
7 Are you from *Argentina* / *Argentinian*?
8 We're from the *UK* / *British*.
9 Are they from *Turkish* / *Türkiye*?
10 We aren't from *Spain* / *Spanish*.
11 She's from *Thai* / *Thailand*.
12 It's the *Japan* / *Japanese* flag.

3 Complete the conversations with a country or nationality from Exercise 1.

1 **A:** Where are you from?
  B: We're from J*apan* .
2 **A:** Are you American?
  B: No, we're A_____ .
3 **A:** Are you from Türkiye?
  B: No, I'm S_____ .
4 **A:** Where is she from?
  B: She's from C_____ .
5 **A:** Are they from the US?
  B: No, they're B_____ .
6 **A:** They're from Mexico.
  B: Wow! We're M_____ , too.

Grammar

be: *you/we/they*

4 Choose the correct alternatives.

1 They <u>*aren't*</u> / *are* from Türkiye. They're Spanish.
2 We *are* / *is* student nurses.
3 They *is* / *are* football players.
4 Who *are* / *am* they?
5 We *isn't* / *aren't* housemates.
6 Where *is* / *are* you from?
7 *Are* / *Is* you a doctor?
8 *Is* / *Are* Sam and I in the same class?

5 Complete the sentences with the correct form of *be*. Use the words in brackets and short forms.

1 They _*aren't British*_ . (not / British).
2 Where _____? (they / from)
3 _____? (you / friends)
4 Who _____? (the boys)
5 We _____. (not / Turkish)
6 Harry and I _____. (not / nurses)

6 Complete the conversations. Use short forms.

1 **A:** Maria and Anna / sisters?
    Are Maria and Anna sisters?
  B: No, / housemates.
    No, they're housemates.

2 **A:** you and Simon / Spanish?

  B: No, / from Argentina.

3 **A:** Who / they?

  B: They / my friends.

4 **A:** we / late?

  B: No, / on time.

English in action

Ask for and give contact information

1 Match questions 1–6 with answers a–f.

1 What's your phone number?   _d_
2 Sorry, can you say that again?   ....
3 What's your name?   ....
4 How do you spell your family name?   ....
5 What's your email address?   ....
6 How do you spell your first name?   ....

a It's Lucia Hernandez.
b It's hernandez.lucia@fastmail.com.
c L-U-C-I-A.
d It's 07781 325 768.
e Yes, 07781 325 768.
f H-E-R-N-A-N-D-E-Z.

2 Correct the questions.

1 ~~What~~ your first name?
   ***What's** your first name?*
2 What's you family name?
   ....
3 How's your phone number?
   ....
4 What's your email number?
   ....
5 How you spell that?
   ....
6 Me family name is Demir.
   ....
7 My phone number are 07820 511 370.
   ....
8 Sorry, can your say that again?
   ....

3 Write questions for these answers. Use short forms.

1 *What's your name?*
   It's Jane Bernard.
2 ....
   J-A-N-E.
3 ....
   B-E-R-N-A-R-D.
4 ....
   It's 07110 331 288.
5 ....
   Yes, 07110 331 228.
6 ....
   It's jane_bernand@mymail.com.

Listening

1 🔊 1.01 Listen to three conversations. Match conversations 1–3 with the places.

a hospital   ....
a language school   ....
an international conference   ....

2 Listen again. Tick (✓) the jobs you hear.

student	✓	manager	☐
nurse	☐	taxi driver	☐
doctor	☐	teacher	☐
football player	☐	office worker	☐
pilot	☐	farmer	☐

3a Complete the table.

Name	Nationality	Job
Lucia	Argentinian	student
Gosia	Polish	
Maria		
David	Brazilian	
Sarah		student doctor
Pete		
Cristina		manager

b Listen again and check.

4a Are the sentences true (T) or false (F)?

1 Gosia is from Warsaw.   _F_
2 It isn't Lucia's first time in the UK.   ....
3 The teacher is from Canada.   ....
4 It is Maria's first day.   ....
5 Maria is from São Paolo.   ....
6 Pete is from London.   ....
7 Pete is a is teacher at a university in Manchester.   ....
8 Cristina is a manager at a university in Madrid.   ....

b Listen again and check.

Reading

1 Read the webpage. Choose the correct options, a, b or c.

1 Thistle House is a ....
   a university
   b language school
   c hotel
2 It is in ....
   a London
   b Melbourne
   c Edinburgh

2 Write the answers.

1 Who is from South Korea?   *Mi Na*
2 Who is an office worker?   ....
3 Who is Brazilian?   ....
4 Who is Canadian?   ....
5 Who is a pilot?   ....
6 Who is a manager?   ....
7 Who is from New York?   ....
8 Who is British?   ....
9 Who is Italian?   ....
10 Who is a nurse?   ....

3 Are the sentences true (T) or false (F)?

1 Thistle House is a small school.   *F*
2 Edinburgh is in the US.   ....
3 The students come from a lot of different countries.   ....
4 The teachers are all British.   ....
5 The manager is from Edinburgh.   ....
6 Steve and Jenny are both Canadian.   ....
7 Gabriela isn't a teacher.   ....
8 Mi Na and Matteo are students.   ....

4 Read the webpage again. Find six jobs, five countries and two nationalities.

1 Jobs
   student , ...
   teacher , ...
   .... , ...
2 Countries
   .... , *Canada* ,
   .... , ...
3 Nationalities
   .... , *English*

Welcome to Thistle House!

Thistle House is a large English language school. It is in the centre of Edinburgh in the UK. Our students and teachers come from all over the world.

Hi! I'm Lesley. I'm the manager of Thistle House. I'm not from Edinburgh. I'm from London in the UK.

Hello, we're teachers here! I'm Steve. I'm from Vancouver in Canada. Jenny is American. She's from New York.

Hi, I'm Gabriela. I'm from Brazil. I'm an office worker at Thistle House.

Hi, we're students here. I'm Mi Na and I'm from South Korea. Matteo is from Italy. I'm a nurse and Matteo's a pilot.

Writing

1 Read profiles A–D and complete the table.

A

Hi. I'm Sara Demir.
I'm Turkish.
I'm from Istanbul.
I'm a doctor.

B

Hello. I'm Matthew Turner.
I'm from Manchester
in the UK.
I'm an office worker.

C

My name is Sandra
Fernandez. I'm from
Buenos Aires in Argentina.
I'm an English teacher.

D

Hi. I'm Dawid Nowak.
I'm from Warsaw
in Poland.
I'm a taxi driver.

Name	City	Country	Nationality	Job
Sara Demir	Istanbul			
	Manchester			
		Argentina		
			Polish	

2 Read the Focus box. Underline the capital letters in the profiles in Exercise 1. Circle the full stops.

> ### Using capital letters and full stops
> Use capital letters (A, B, C, etc.) at the beginning of a sentence. Use full stops (.) at the end of a sentence.
> *My name is Calum Edwards.*
> *He's from Thailand.*
>
> We also use CAPITAL letters:
> - for *I*: ***I****'m an office worker.*
> - for names: *Her name is **A**lison **S**tewart.*
> - for places: *I'm from **V**ancouver in **C**anada.*
> - for nationalities: *He's **S**panish.*
> - for languages: *I'm an **E**nglish teacher.*

3 Rewrite the sentences with capital letters and full stops.

1 becky isn't from the us she's from canada
   Becky isn't from the US. She's from Canada.

2 my name is peter i'm from london

3 jane and i aren't sisters we're housemates

4 my mother is polish and my father is from italy

5 antoni is a football player

6 jose and pablo are in the same class

4 Write profiles for the two people. Use capital letters and full stops.

1

Name: gloria lopez
City: mexico city
Country: mexico
Job: doctor

2

Name: charlie suparat
City: bangkok
Country: thailand
Job: student

Prepare

5 Complete the information about someone you know (a friend or someone in your family).
Name: ....
City: ....
Country: ....
Job: ....

Write

6 Write a profile using the information in Exercise 5. Use capital letters and full stops.

....

....

....

....

2A

Vocabulary

Family

1 Put the letters in the correct order to make family words.

1 hteomr _____mother_____
2 mmu _____
3 nso _____
4 aetrfh _____
5 hnsuadb _____
6 add _____
7 srtise _____
8 hbertor _____
9 rhutdaeg _____
10 ewif _____

2 Write the family words from Exercise 1.

♂		♀	
1	_father_	6	_mother_
2		7	
3		8	
4		9	
5		10	

3 Complete the sentences with a word from Exercise 1.

1 My h_usband_ is from Türkiye.
2 My b_____ is a teacher.
3 Her s_____'s name is Beth.
4 Their f_____ is Argentinian.
5 My m_____ is from Japan.
6 His w_____'s name is Luisa.
7 Their d_____ is a doctor.
8 Their s_____'s name is Pablo.

Grammar

Possessive 's, I/my, you/your, etc.

4 Choose the correct alternatives.

1 They / _Their_ mother's name is Sylvia.
2 Jacob's / Jacob dad is a teacher.
3 We / Our mum is Mexican.
4 George / George's wife is from Spain.
5 This is my dog. Its / Their name is Sparky.
6 My brother is a doctor. His / Her wife is a doctor, too.
7 My son's / son name is Michael.
8 My sister is in Krakow now. Her / His husband is Polish.

5 Rewrite the sentences. Use the possessive 's.

1 My mother mother is from Argentina.
  My mother's mother is from Argentina.
2 Lucy is Daniel sister.
  _____
3 My cat name is Pixie.
  _____
4 Oliver wife is a nurse.
  _____
5 His daughter name is Elizabeth.
  _____
6 Sandra is Jon wife.
  _____
7 My husband mother and father are farmers.
  _____
8 What's your friend name?
  _____

6 Complete the sentences with the possessive adjective of the word in brackets.

1 Is that your sister? What's ___her___ name? (she)
2 _____ family are from the US. (we)
3 My brother is a student. _____ wife is, too. (he)
4 Carmen and Pilar are Spanish. _____ family is from Madrid. (they)
5 That's my dog. _____ name is Rex. (it)
6 What's _____ name? (you)
7 _____ mother's name is Agata. (I)
8 That's Sara's mother. _____ name's Eve. (she)

2B

Vocabulary

Everyday objects (1)

1 Complete the words for everyday objects.

1	t a b l e ☐	7	d _ s _ ☐
2	c _ a _ r ☐	8	c _ m _ u _ e _ ☐
3	p _ _ n _ ✓	9	k _ _ ☐
4	p _ _ ☐	10	ph _ t _ ☐
5	c _ o _ _ ☐	11	b _ _ k ☐
6	c _ _ ☐	12	b _ x ☐

2 What is in the photo? Tick (✓) the everyday objects in Exercise 1.

3 Write the everyday objects.

1 It's a _____

2 It's a _____

3 It's a _____

4 It's a _____

5 It's a _____

6 It's a _____

Grammar

this, that, these and *those*

4 Rewrite the sentences using *these*.

1 It's a desk.
These are desks.

2 It's a chair.

3 It's a photo.

4 It's a watch.

5 It's a key.

6 It's a box.

7 It's a phone.

8 It's a family.

5 Complete the table with *these* and *that*.

	Near (here)	Far (there)
Singular	this	
Plural		those

6 Choose the correct alternatives.

1 *This / These* are my keys.
2 Are *these / this* your books?
3 Is *this / that* your father there?
4 *That / Those* is my desk.
5 What's in *this / those* box?
6 *Those / This* is Sofi's cup.
7 Is *this / these* your chair?
8 *Those / That* aren't my keys.
9 Is *that / these* John's computer?
10 Is *that / those* your sister?

7 Complete the sentences with *this, these, that* or *those*.

1 ____This____ is my sister, Jane.
2 Are _____ your keys in my bag?
3 Is _____ your car in the street over there?
4 Are _____ Sam's books on his desk?

Vocabulary

Numbers 1–100

1 Match the numbers with the words.

12	twenty
14	thirteen
16	eleven
11	twelve
19	fourteen
18	sixteen
13	seventeen
20	fifteen
15	nineteen
17	eighteen

2 Write a word next to each number.

a hundred	eleven	fifteen	~~fifty~~	nineteen	ninety	seventeen
seventy	thirteen	thirty	twelve	twenty		

1	50	_fifty_	7	30	
2	12		8	11	
3	13		9	17	
4	100		10	19	
5	15		11	20	
6	90		12	70	

3 Write the names and ages of six friends or people in your family.

1 ....
2 ....
3 ....
4 ....
5 ....
6 ....

Grammar

Question words with *be*

4 Complete the questions with a question word in the box.

How	What	Where	Who

1 _What_'s his job?
2 .... old is your sister?
3 .... are you from?
4 ....'s your name?
5 .... old are they?
6 ....'s your phone number?
7 .... are those people over there?
8 .... are they from?

5 Match the questions in Exercise 4 with these answers.

1 _Where are they from?_
   They're from Japan.
2 ....
   He's a farmer.
3 ....
   I'm from Türkiye.
4 ....
   They're 11.
5 ....
   It's Maya.
6 ....
   She's 42.
7 ....
   07403 837 383.
8 ....
   They're my friends.

6 Correct the question words.

1 ~~How's~~ your name?
   What's your name?
2 Who are they from?
   ....
3 What old are you?
   ....
4 What's your best friend?
   ....
5 Who's his job?
   ....
6 Where's your house number?
   ....

English in action

Pay for things in a shop

1 Match the sentence halves.

1	How much is	a	is that?
2	Here	b	is £27.99, please.
3	Can I pay	c	those cups?
4	Cash	d	this book?
5	How much	e	by card?
6	How much are	f	my card.
7	Here's your	g	change.
8	That	h	or card?
9	Here's	i	you are.
10	It's	j	£12.

2 Complete the table with the phrases from Exercise 1.

Customer's phrases	Shop assistant's phrases
How much is that?	*It's £12.*

3 Complete the two conversations with the words in the box.

> change   card   ~~help~~   here   much   that   those

1 A: Hi, can I ¹ _____help_____ you?
  B: Yes, please. How ² _____ is this cup?
  A: It's £5.99.
  B: And how much are ³ _____ pens?
  A: £1.
  B: OK. Two cups and two pens please. How much is ⁴ _____ ?
  A: That's £13.98, please. Cash or ⁵ _____ ?
  B: Cash, please. ⁶ _____ you are.
  A: Thank you. And here's your ⁷ _____ .
  B: Thank you.

> card   excuse   how   it's   pay   that's   you

2 A: ⁸ _____ me. How much is this?
  B: The desk? ⁹ _____ £90.
  A: And ¹⁰ _____ much is the chair?
  B: It's £30.
  A: OK. The desk and the chair, please.
  B: ¹¹ _____ £120, please.
  A: Can I ¹² _____ by card?
  B: Yes, of course.
  A: Here ¹³ _____ are.
  B: Thank you. Here's your ¹⁴ _____ .
  A: Thank you.

Listening

1 🔊 2.01 **Listen to the podcast. Where are the people from? Choose the correct option, a or b.**

1 Maija
  a Poland
  b Thailand

2 Kevin
  a London, in the UK
  b New York, in the US

3 Amelia
  a Argentina
  b Canada

2 Listen again. Number the objects in the order you hear them.

  _1_ phone
  ____ camera
  ____ computer
  ____ photos
  ____ credit card
  ____ cash
  ____ book
  ____ passport
  ____ keys

3 Match the people (1–3) with the objects in their bags (a–c).

1 Maija ____
2 Kevin ____
3 Amelia ____

a a book, a computer, keys, cash
b a phone, a passport, a camera, cash, photos
c a phone, keys, a credit card, a book

2

Reading

A

B

C

1 Read the article. Match photos A–C with the people.

Kelly _____   Sara _____   Yui _____

2 Are the sentences true (T) or false (F)?

1 Sara's family is big. _____
2 Sara's dad is British. _____
3 Sara's sisters are both students. _____
4 Yui's family is Japanese. _____
5 Yui's daughter is five years old. _____
6 Yui's brother is a teacher in the US. _____
7 Kelly's family is small. _____
8 Kelly's husband is called Brian. _____

3 Complete the sentences with the words in the box.

| children | daughter | father | husband | mother | parents' |
| sister | son | | | | |

1 Sara's _____ names are Eduardo and Laura.
2 Sara's _____ is a nurse.
3 Sara's _____ is from the UK.
4 Yui's _____'s name is Riku.
5 Yui's _____ is 67.
6 Kelly's _____ is from Italy.
7 Kelly's _____'s names are Louise and Nathan.
8 Kelly's _____ is eight years old.

4 Underline all the numbers in the article. Write them in order from low to high.

_____

_____

_____

Who's in your family?

Hi, I'm Sara. I'm from Madrid in Spain, but now I'm a student in London. My family is very big! My parents' names are Eduardo and Laura. My dad is from Spain, but my mum isn't Spanish. She's from the UK. This is a photo of my brothers and sisters. My sisters' names are Lucia and Nuria. Lucia's 26 and Nuria's 21. My brothers' names are David, Pablo and Alex. They are 24, 22 and 18. Lucia's a nurse and David's a teacher. Nuria, Pablo and Alex are students.

This is my favourite photo of my family. We're from Japan. I'm Yui. I'm 37. That's my son. His name's Riku. He's 5 years old. My brother's name is Haruki. He's 30. He's a doctor in the US now.
My mother's name is Mei. She's 65. My father's name is Ryo. He's 67.

I'm Kelly. I'm from Canada. My family isn't very big. My mum's name is Jenny and my dad's name is Brian. They're 70 years old. My husband's name is Damien. He's from Italy. Those are our children. Our daughter's name is Louise. She's 8 years old. Our son's name is Nathan. He's 6.

Writing

1 Read the conversation. Choose the correct alternatives.

A: Hello. Welcome to Cambridge English School. What's your name?

B: Marcin Kowalski

A: How do you spell your first name?

B: M-A-R-C-I-N.

A: And how do you spell your family name?

B: K-O-W-A-L-S-K-I.

A: Where are you from, Marcin?

B: I'm from Lodz, in Poland.

A: What's your date of birth?

B: It's 22/07/89.

A: Thanks. And what's your job?

B: I'm a pilot.

A: OK. And what's your address in the UK?

B: It's 22 River Street, Cambridge, CB12 1AR.

A: Thank you. And what's your phone number?

B: It's 07329 876 345.

A: And what's your email address?

B: It's m.kowalski@webmail.com.

A: Thank you.

1 The student's *first name / family name* is Marcin.

2 He is from *Cambridge / Lodz*.

3 His *postcode / date of birth* is 22/07/89.

4 He is a *farmer / pilot*.

5 His address is *22 River Street / River Road*.

6 His *email address / postcode* is CB12 1AR.

2 Read the Focus box. Write Marcin's date of birth.

....

Completing forms

- surname = family name
- DOB = date of birth
- occupation = job
- Write your address in this order:
  house number + street name, city, postcode
- Write your date of birth in this order:
  DD/MM/YY = date/month/year

3 Complete the form with the words in the box.

> address   DOB   email address   first name
> occupation   phone number   signature   surname

Cambridge English School	Student registration form
1	Hana
2	Matsumoto
3	17 Sylvan Street, Cambridge, CB1 5JX
4	07892 321 465
5	h_matsumoto@webmail.com
6	21/05/95
7	teacher
8	Hana Matsumoto

Prepare

4 Complete the form with the information in the box.

> 12/08/1988   07343 211 498
> 330 Queen Street, Cambridge, CB12 2ED   Rob Schmidt
> schmidt.rr@abcmail.com   taxi driver

Cambridge English School	Student registration form
First name	1
Surname	2
Address	3
Phone number	4
Email address	5
DOB	6
Occupation	7
Signature	Rob Schmidt

Write

5 Complete the form with information about someone in your family.

Cambridge English School	Student registration form
First name	
Surname	
Address	
Phone number	
Email address	
DOB	
Occupation	
Signature	

Vocabulary

Places in town

1 Complete the places in town. Then complete the crossword.

Across

2 f l a t
5 h _ _ s _
7 c _ n _ m _
8 p _ r _
10 h _ t _ l
11 s _ _ e _ m _ _ k _ t
12 r _ s _ au _ _ nt

Down

1 c a f é
3 t _ _ in s _ at _ _ n
4 b _ o _ sh _ p
6 m _ r _ e _
9 b _ _ k

2 Write the places in town.

1 _____ 2 _____ 3 _____

4 _____ 5 _____ 6 _____

Grammar

There is/ There are; singular and plural nouns

3 Choose the correct alternatives.

1 *There is / There are* two Mexican restaurants in my town.
2 *There aren't / There isn't* any hotels.
3 *There is / There are* three train stations in this town.
4 *There aren't / There isn't* a cinema.
5 *There are / There is* a supermarket.
6 *There are / There is* no restaurants.
7 *There isn't / There aren't* a park in my town.
8 *There are / There is* two banks.
9 *There aren't / There isn't* any houses in the town centre.
10 *There is / There are* a market.

4 Put the words in the correct order to make sentences.

1 a cinema / There / is
There is a cinema.
2 are / two / There / bookshops
_____
3 aren't / parks / any / There
_____
4 a bank / There / my / isn't / town/ in
_____
5 aren't / in / There / hotels / town / any / my
_____
6 no / There / supermarkets / here / are
_____
7 train stations / aren't / town / my / any / There / in
_____
8 my / four / town / There / cafés / are / in
_____

5 Complete the descriptions with *there is, there are, there isn't* or *there aren't.*

In my town **1** _____ two parks and a big market. **2** _____ four cafés and three restaurants. **3** _____ a supermarket. **4** _____ any bookshops.

My town is great! **5** _____ a cinema and a park. **6** _____ are two restaurants – a Thai restaurant and an Argentinian restaurant. **7** _____ two supermarkets and a market. **8** _____ no banks and no train stations.

Vocabulary

Rooms and things in a home

1 Complete the table with the words in the box.

bathroom	bed	bedroom	kitchen	lift	living room	oven
shower	sofa	table	toilet	TV		

Rooms in a house	Things in a house
	toilet

2 Write the rooms.

1 _____

2 _____

3 _____

4 _____

3 Write the things in a home you can see in Exercise 2.

Room 1: *sofa,* _____
Room 2: _____
Room 3: _____
Room 4: _____

4 Complete the sentences with words from Exercise 1.

1 There's a shower and a t*oilet* _____ in the bathroom.
2 Is there an oven in the k_____?
3 How many b_____ are in the bedroom?
4 There's a sofa and a TV in the l_____ room.
5 The flat is on the 10th floor, but there's a l_____ .
6 Is there a t_____ in the kitchen?

Grammar

Is there a/ an ...? / Are there any ...?

5 Choose the correct alternatives.

1 *Is there / There is* a living room?
2 How many bedrooms *is there / are there*?
3 How many *rooms / room* are there in your flat?
4 *Is there / Are there* any lifts?
5 *Is there / Are there* wifi in the flat?
6 *Is there / Are there* a shower in the bathroom?
7 *Are there / Is there* any shops near your flat?
8 How many *floor / floors* are there?

6 Match questions 1–8 in Exercise 5 with answers a–h.

_1_ a No, there isn't, but there's a TV and a sofa in the kitchen.
____ b There are only two rooms. It's small.
____ c No, there aren't, but my flat is on the 1st floor.
____ d There are three bedrooms and six beds.
____ e Yes, there is. It's in all the rooms.
____ f Yes, there are. There are two supermarkets and a bookshop.
____ g Yes, there is. There's a shower and a bath.
____ h There are eight. My flat is on the 6th floor.

7 Complete the conversation with the correct form of *there is* or *there are*. Use short forms.

A: How many rooms are there in your flat?
B: 1 _There are_ five. 2 _____ a kitchen, bathroom, living room and two bedrooms.
A: 3 _____ a TV in the living room?
B: Yes, 4 _____ .
A: And 5 _____ wifi?
B: No 6 _____ .
A: What floor is your flat on?
B: It's on the 2nd floor.
A: 7 _____ a lift?
B: No, 8 _____ .
A: 9 _____ any restaurants near your flat?
B: Yes, 10 _____ . There's a Spanish restaurant and a Brazilian café.

3c

Vocabulary

Describing places

1 Put the letters in the correct order to make words to describe places.

1 gib   _big_
2 ituqe   _____
3 llsam   _____
4 evnxpeesi   _____
5 pceah   _____
6 dab   _____
7 ysub   _____
8 wne   _____
9 dogo   _____
10 odl   _____

2 Complete the pairs of opposites in the table with words from Exercise 1.

old	_new_
	busy
good	
	cheap
big	

3 Complete the sentences.

1 Amy's flat isn't big. It's ___small___ .
2 This hotel isn't new. It's _____ .
3 The café isn't busy. It's _____ .
4 This restaurant isn't cheap. It's _____ .
5 That supermarket isn't good. It's _____ .
6 My town isn't small. It's _____ .
7 The university isn't old. It's _____ .
8 The train station isn't quiet. It's _____ .
9 That hotel isn't expensive. It's _____ .
10 The food isn't bad. It's _____ .

Grammar

Position of adjectives

4 Correct the sentences.

1 Is there a park big?
   Is there a big park?
2 That is a bookshop good.
   _____
3 There are two supermarkets new.
   _____
4 My flat small is.
   _____
5 There's a market busy.
   _____
6 It is a restaurant bad.
   _____
7 This is a town quiet.
   _____
8 There aren't any restaurants expensive.
   _____
9 Is there cheap a hotel in this town?
   _____
10 Are there any houses old in this town?
   _____

5 Put the words in the correct order to make sentences or questions.

1 cinema / old / is / That
   That cinema is old.
2 busy / train station / is / The
   _____
3 restaurant / that / Is / expensive ?
   _____
4 bank / Is / the / small ?
   _____
5 new / not / The / is / bookshop
   _____
6 any / supermarkets / there / cheap / Are ?
   _____
7 your / Is / big / town's / market ?
   _____
8 town / the / big / your / Is / in / park ?
   _____
9 is / Simon's / big / not / flat
   _____
10 in / good / town / Are / hotels / your/ there / any ?
   _____

English in action
Ask for and give directions

1 Complete the conversations with the words in the box.

| at   down   ~~near~~   on   one   past |

A: Excuse me. Is there a bank **1** _near_ here?
B: Yes, there's **2** _____ on Main Street. Go **3** _____
Park Road, go **4** _____ the university and turn
left **5** _____ the cinema. The bank is **6** _____
the right.
A: Thank you.
B: No problem.

| after   down   on   straight   where's |

A: Excuse me. **7** _____ the train station, please?
B: The train station? It's **8** _____ Station Road.
Go **9** _____ on then turn right **10** _____ the
supermarket. Go **11** _____ Station Road and the
train station is on the left.
A: Thank you very much.
B: You're welcome.

2 Put the words in the correct order to make sentences and questions.

1 there / supermarket / here / Is / a / near ?
   Is there a supermarket near here?

2 cinema / past / Go / the
   _____

3 down / South Street / Go
   _____

4 on / a / There's / Station Road / bank
   _____

5 left / at / the / Turn / park
   _____

6 past / school / Go / the
   _____

7 restaurant / the / on / right / The / is
   _____

8 next / park / It's / to / a
   _____

Listening

1 🔊 3.01 Listen to people talk about their towns. How many towns are big?
one / two / three

2 Listen and tick (✓) the words you hear.

hospital	✓
Thai restaurant	☐
computer shop	☐
park	☐
bookshop	☐
supermarket	☐
train station	☐
Spanish restaurant	☐
university	☐
hotel	☐
houses	☐
café	☐
bank	☐
offices	☐

3a Choose the correct alternatives.
Speaker 1
1 There is a Turkish restaurant and a _Mexican_ / *Spanish* restaurant.
2 The cinema is *small / big*.
3 The Japanese restaurant is *cheap / expensive*.
4 The park is next to the *hospital / school*.

Speaker 2
5 There aren't any *cafés / restaurants*.
6 There's a *market / supermarket* on Main Street.
7 The cinema *is / isn't* new.
8 *There's / There isn't* a train station.

Speaker 3
9 There *are / aren't* big offices.
10 There's a *school / university* and a hospital.
11 The parks are *big / small*.
12 It's a *quiet / busy* town.

b Listen again and check.

4 Listen and write the adjectives you hear.
Speaker 1
great, big, good
_____

Speaker 2
_____
_____

Speaker 3
_____
_____

Reading

1 What is in the photo? Choose the place you see.

a a cinema   b a train station   c a hotel

2 Read the descriptions of hotels. Match them with the adverts.

Grand Hotel				
Rooms:	small	0 ▇▇▇▇▇ 5	big
Bathrooms:	old	0 ▇ 5	new
Area:	busy	0 ▇▇▇▇ 5	quiet
Wifi:	bad	0 ▇ 5	good
Price:	cheap	0 ▇▇ 5	expensive

Metro Hotel				
Rooms:	small	0 ▇▇▇ 5	big
Bathrooms:	old	0 ▇▇▇▇▇ 5	new
Area:	busy	0 ▇ 5	quiet
Wifi:	bad	0 ▇▇▇▇▇ 5	good
Price:	cheap	0 ▇▇▇▇ 5	expensive

City Flat				
Rooms:	small	0 ▇ 5	big
Bathrooms:	old	0 ▇▇▇ 5	new
Area:	busy	0 ▇▇▇ 5	quiet
Wifi:	bad	0 ▇▇▇ 5	good
Price:	cheap	0 ▇▇▇▇▇ 5	expensive

1 ....
There are six bedrooms and seven bathrooms. The bedrooms are small, but the beds are new. The bathrooms are new. It's next to the train station and market. There is wifi in the bedrooms. It is £80 a night.

2 ....
There are two bedrooms and one bathroom. The bathroom is new. There isn't a shower in the bathroom. There is a kitchen with an oven but there isn't a living room. It is near cafés and restaurants. There is wifi in the kitchen. It is £100 a night.

3 ....
There are 20 big bedrooms and 21 bathrooms. The bathrooms are very old. There aren't any showers in the bathrooms. It is near a small park and a bookshop. There is no wifi in the hotel. It is £40 a night.

3 Are the sentences true (T) or false (F)?

1 There are 20 bathrooms in the Grand Hotel.   *F*

2 The bedrooms are big in the Grand Hotel.   ....

3 The Grand Hotel is near a supermarket.   ....

4 The Grand Hotel is £60 a night.   ....

5 There are six bedrooms and six bathrooms in the Metro Hotel.   ....

6 The beds in the Metro Hotel are old.   ....

7 The bathrooms in the Metro Hotel are not old.   ....

8 There are two bathrooms in the City Flat.   ....

9 There isn't a shower in the bathroom in the City Flat.   ....

10 There is wifi in the bedrooms in the Metro Hotel.   ....

4 Choose the correct alternatives.

1 There *is* / *isn't* a train station near the Grand Hotel.

2 There *is* / *isn't* wifi in the Grand Hotel.

3 There *are* / *aren't any* showers in the Grand Hotel bathrooms.

4 There *is* / *isn't* a supermarket next to the Metro Hotel.

5 There *is* / *isn't* wifi in the Metro Hotel.

6 There *is* / *isn't* a living room in the City Flat.

7 There *is* / *isn't* a kitchen in the City Flat.

8 There *are* / *aren't any* restaurants near the City Flat.

5 Complete the table with words from the descriptions of the three hotels.

Rooms in the house
bedroom

Things in the house
bed

Places in town
café

3

Writing

1 Read the descriptions and choose the correct answer, a or b.

My home

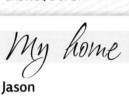

Jason

My house is old, but it is very big. It's next to the park and it's very quiet. There are four bedrooms, a living room, a kitchen and a bathroom. In the kitchen there is a table and there are four chairs. In the living room there is a sofa and a chair. There's a clock, but there isn't a TV. In the bathroom there's a bath and a shower. My bedroom is small. There is a bed and an old chair.

Jane

My flat is in the town centre on a busy street. It's new, but it's very small. There's a kitchen, a bedroom and a bathroom. There isn't a living room, but there's a sofa and a TV in the kitchen. In the bathroom there's a toilet and a shower, but there isn't a bath. In the bedroom there's a bed and a chair. My flat is on the 12th floor, but there is a lift.

1 Jason's house is _____ .
   (a) big   **b** small
2 His house is next to a _____ .
   a supermarket   **b** park
3 There are _____ bedrooms in Jason's house.
   a three   **b** four
4 There isn't a _____ in Jason's living room.
   a sofa   **b** TV
5 Jane's flat is on a _____ street.
   a busy   **b** quiet
6 Her flat is _____ .
   a old   **b** new
7 There's a sofa and TV in the _____ in Jane's flat.
   a bedroom   **b** kitchen
8 There isn't a _____ in Jane's bathroom.
   a bath   **b** shower

2 Read the Focus box. Underline examples of *and* and *but* in Exercise 1.

Using *and* and *but*

Join sentences with *and* and *but*.
Use *and* to add information.
   *My house is big. It's old. → My house is big **and** old.*
Use *but* to give opposite or different information.
   There isn't a sofa. There is a chair. →
   *There isn't a sofa, **but** there is a chair.*
   There is a bath. There isn't a shower. →
   *There is a bath, **but** there isn't a shower.*

---

3 Correct the sentences.
1 There is a big kitchen, but there is a big living room.
   There is a big kitchen and there is a big living room.
2 There isn't a bath in the bathroom and there's a shower.
3 There's a market, but there's a supermarket.
4 The market is very good, but it's cheap.
5 There isn't a TV and there's a radio.
6 There are two bedrooms but there is a living room.

4 Match the sentence halves.
1 There isn't a sofa in the living room, but   _d_
2 There is a Thai restaurant and   _____
3 There's a computer in the bedroom, but   _____
4 In Will's flat there's a big kitchen, but   _____
5 Andy's house is big. There are two living rooms and   _____
6 There isn't a bedroom, but   _____

a there isn't wifi.
b there isn't a living room.
c six bedrooms.
d there is an armchair.
e there's a bed in the living room.
f a Mexican restaurant next to my flat.

Prepare

5 Make notes about your house or flat.

Rooms (e.g. kitchen)	Things (e.g. sofa)	Old? New? Good? Bad?

Write

6 Write a description of your house or flat. Use *and* and *but*.

_____

_____

_____

_____

_____

_____

Vocabulary

Describing people

1 Complete the words.

1 This is Elin.
She's ¹i _ h _ _
2 _ _. She's got
green eyes and
²b _ _ _ _ hair.

2 This is Richard.
He's in his 50s.
He's got ³b _ _ _
eyes and
⁴g _ _ _ hair.

3 This is Avi.
He's ⁵i _ h _ _
3 _ _. He's got
brown hair and
a ⁶b _ _ _ _.

2 Complete the crossword.

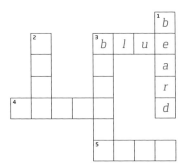

Down

1 My father has got a long grey ___beard___.
2 Sam has got long _____.
3 Adam hasn't got brown hair. He's got
_____ hair.

Across

3 Anna has got blonde hair and ___blue___
eyes.
4 She's got beautiful _____ eyes.
5 He's got brown hair and green _____.

Grammar

Have/Has got

3 Choose the correct alternatives.

1 I *have got* / *has got* long hair.
2 Kate *haven't got* / *hasn't got* green hair!
3 Jon *have got* / *has got* blue eyes.
4 We *haven't got* / *hasn't got* short hair.
5 Mike *have got* / *has got* two daughters.
6 I *has got* / *have got* two sisters.
7 Sarah *has got* / *have got* a small house.
8 We *have got* / *has got* a black cat.

4 Make sentences using the prompts. Use short forms.

1 Sophie / not / got / a phone.
   Sophie hasn't got a phone.

2 I / not / got / a pen.

3 We / got / a big house.

4 They / not / got / any books.

5 David / got / four / dogs.

6 My desk / not / got / a chair.

7 Sonia / got / a black car.

8 Isobel / not / got / a watch.

5 Write sentences using the information in the table. Use short forms.

	+	−
I	blue eyes	brown hair
Rob	blonde hair	green hair
Eva	a bed	a sofa
Matt's town	a cinema	a market
My husband and I	a small house	a clock
Andy and Tim	a big flat	a table

1 I *'ve got blue eyes* .
   I *haven't got brown hair* .
2 Rob _____ .
   He _____ .
3 Eva _____ .
   She _____ .
4 Matt's town _____ .
   It _____ .
5 My husband and I _____ .
   We _____ .
6 Andy and Tim _____ .
   They _____ .

4B

Vocabulary

Everyday objects (2)

1 Complete the words for everyday objects.
1 p a s s p o r t
2 b _ _
3 b _ t _ le o _ w _ t _ _
4 f _ _ d
5 c _ _ d _ _ c _ _ d
6 t _ c k _ _ s
7 h _ _ s _ k _ _ s
8 c _ _ e _ a
9 s _ _ g _ _ _ _ e _
10 p _ _ n _
11 c _ _ t
12 m _ _ _ y

2 Choose the correct alternatives.

1 a map / *a newspaper*

2 money / a credit card

3 a passport / a ticket

4 a coat / a bag

5 a camera / a phone

6 food / a bottle of water

Grammar

Have/Has got: questions

3 Complete the conversations with *have* or *has got*.
1 **A:** _Have_ we _got_ a map?
　B: No, we _haven't_ .
2 **A:** _____ you _____ any tickets?
　B: Yes, I _____ .
3 **A:** _____ they _____ any food?
　B: Yes, they _____ .
4 **A:** _____ Jane _____ a credit card?
　B: No, she _____ .
5 **A:** _____ they _____ any children?
　B: Yes, they _____ .
6 **A:** _____ the dog _____ its ball?
　B: Yes, it _____ .

4 Correct the sentences.
1 ~~Has~~ you got your passport?
　Have you got your passport?
2 You have got a ticket?
3 Has she a new camera?
4 **A:** Has John got a bottle of water?
　B: Yes, he's got.
5 Is Susan got food?
6 Has they got their coats?
7 **A:** Have you got brothers or sisters?
　B: No, I haven't got.
8 Have you get a new phone?

5 Write questions and short answers with *have* or *has got*.
1 George / new coat (no)
　Has George got a new coat?
　No, he hasn't.
2 your flat / a lift (yes)
3 you / brothers or sisters (no)
4 you / the tickets (yes)
5 they / a big house (no)
6 he / an expensive camera (yes)

Vocabulary

Common verbs

1 Complete the phrases with verbs from the box.

buy	drink	go	see	~~take~~	take	try	visit

1 _____take_____ photos
2 _____ tea
3 _____ a museum
4 _____ to a market
5 _____ a show
6 _____ Mexican food
7 _____ a black taxi
8 _____ a new camera

2 Choose the correct option, a or b.

1 Don't _____ to the car museum. It isn't interesting.
   a visit   **ⓑ** go
2 Don't _____ a film. Go to a show.
   a try   b see
3 _____ tea in London. It's very nice.
   a Visit   b Drink
4 _____ Turkish food. There is lots of good Turkish food in London.
   a Try   b Take
5 _____ the British Museum. It's very big.
   a Go   b Visit
6 _____ a coat and an umbrella to London.
   a Take   b Go
7 _____ some nice things in the shops.
   a Buy   b See
8 _____ lots of photos.
   a See   b Take

Grammar

Imperatives

3 Match the sentence halves.

1 Don't go   _b_
2 Walk! Don't   _____
3 Don't speak Turkish to her,   _____
4 Put your cup   _____
5 Don't eat   _____
6 Don't take   _____
7 Don't talk   _____
8 Ask me   _____

a in the kitchen please.
b to Japan now.
c food in the cinema.
d to your friends in class.
e run!
f for help.
g photos in the museum, please.
h she's Italian

4 Correct the sentences.

1 Don't ~~visits~~ Buckingham Palace!
   Don't **visit** Buckingham Palace!
2 Drinks lots of water!
   _____
3 Doesn't buy coffee there. It's expensive!
   _____
4 Don't goes to that supermarket. It's very busy.
   _____
5 Not visit the town. It's not good for holidays.
   _____
6 Sees that show. It's very good!
   _____
7 Not try the tea in that restaurant.
   _____
8 Takes lots of photos!
   _____

5 Complete the sentences with the correct form of the verbs from the box.

~~buy~~	drink	see	take	talk	try

1 _____Don't buy_____ that camera. It isn't very good. ✗
2 _____ water next to your computer! ✗
3 _____ that film. It's great! ✓
4 _____ Spanish food. It's very nice. ✓
5 _____ in the cinema! ✗
6 _____ a photo! ✓

English in action

Tell the time

1 Match the times in the box with sentences 1–10.

16.15	05.30	07.40	18.45	11.00	03.50	14.10	12.20
~~09.35~~	01.05						

1 It's twenty-five to ten. *09.35*
2 It's quarter to seven. _____
3 It's half past five. _____
4 It's twenty past twelve. _____
5 It's ten past two. _____
6 It's quarter past four. _____
7 It's twenty to eight. _____
8 It's eleven o'clock. _____
9 It's five past one. _____
10 It's ten to four. _____

2 Write the times from Exercise 1.

1 It's _____ .
2 It's _____ .
3 It's _____ .

4 It's _____ .
5 It's _____ .
6 It's _____ .

3 Complete the conversations with the words in the box. There is one extra word for each conversation.

half	it	late	o'clock

A: What time is **1** _____ ?
B: It's three **2** _____ .
A: Oh no! I'm **3** _____ !

at	on	seven	six	time

A: What **4** _____ is the train to Edinburgh?
B: It's **5** _____ quarter to seven.
A: **6** _____ fifteen?
B: No, **7** _____ forty-five.

is	past	thirty	to

A: What time **8** _____ the next bus?
B: It's at half **9** _____ two.
A: Two **10** _____ ?
B: Yes.

Listening

1 Label the photos with *airport* and *hotel*.

a _____

b _____

2  4.01 Listen to the conversation. Where is Uncle Joe?

_____

3 Listen again and complete the description of Uncle Joe.
1 He's got a _____ .
2 He's got _____ eyes.
3 He's about _____ years old.
4 He's got _____ hair.
5 He's got a _____ coat.

4 Choose the correct photo of Uncle Joe (A or B).

 A ☐

 B ☐

Reading

1 Look at the photo and read the email. Where is Mike's work trip?

From: Yoshi26@email.com
To: MikeD@abcnet.com
Subject: Tips for Tokyo

Hi Mike, how are you? I'm OK. I'm always very busy at work, but I like my new job. How's your job at Telefónica?

So, you've got a work trip to Tokyo? Great! It's a good city to visit. Here is some information to help you in Tokyo.

¹Take the metro. It's not expensive, and the Tokyo metro is big. There are stations everywhere. Taxis are expensive. Don't take them.

²Visit Asakusa. There's a beautiful temple there. Also, ³go to Harajuku Park on a Sunday. There are lots of interesting people there – take your camera!

Try Japanese food. ⁴Go to an izakaya (a Japanese café) and eat some gyoza. ⁵Drink some sake or green tea.

⁶Take a coat. Tokyo is cold in January.

Mike, have you got a hotel? I live in the Shinjuku area. It's in the centre of Tokyo. Come and stay with me?

Take care and see you soon!

Yoshi

2 Read the email again. Match tips 1–6 with photos A–F.

A

B

C

D

E

F

3 Read the email again and answer the questions.

1 Who lives in the centre of Tokyo?

2 Who has got a very busy job?

3 Which form of transport is not cheap?

4 Which two places are good to take photos?

5 What is gyoza?

6 When is Mike's work trip?

4

Writing

1 Read Magda's email. Are the sentences true (T) or false (F)?

> ● ● ●
>
> Hi Magda,
>
> How are you? Have you got everything for our holiday? I've got a new passport and Jenny's got lots of new clothes. She's got a new coat, trousers, two new shirts, three T-shirts and sunglasses. We've got American money, but we haven't got a credit card. Have you got a credit card? Have you got a camera? Jenny's camera is very old and I haven't got one. I've got my sister's book about New York, but I haven't got a map. Have you got a map?
>
> See you soon,
>
> Alicia

1 Alicia hasn't got a passport.   _F_
2 Jenny's got a new coat and sunglasses. ....
3 Alicia and Jenny have got American money. ....
4 Alicia and Jenny have got a credit card. ....
5 Jenny hasn't got a camera. ....
6 Alicia has got a book about New York and a map. ....

2 Read the Focus box. Circle one example of each type of punctuation in the email in Exercise 1.

Using basic punctuation

Use full stops (.) for sentences:
   I haven't got a map.
Use question marks (?) for questions:
   Have you got a camera?
Use commas (,) in lists:
   She's got a new coat, trousers, two new shirts, three T-shirts and sunglasses.
Use apostrophes (') for missing letters:
   I've got a new passport … .
   (= I have got a new passport … .)
Use apostrophes (') for possessives:
   Jenny's camera is very old … .

3 Correct the sentences.

1 I've got a book, a map a camera and a passport.
   I've got a book, a map, a camera and a passport.
2 Have you got the tickets.

   _____

3 Kirstys coat is black.

   _____

4 Laura hasnt got a computer.

   _____

5 I've got a letter, but I haven't got a stamp

   _____

6 Weve got some food and water.

   _____

4 Add capital letters and punctuation to the email.

hi alicia

how are you im great ive got some american money and my mums credit card i havent got a camera but my phones got a good camera ive got a map of new york city a map of the subway and a map of the airport ive got a bag for the plane with some food water a book and a newspaper

see you next week

magda

Prepare

5 Think of six things to take on a weekend holiday in London. Make a list.

   _____

   _____

   _____

   _____

   _____

Write

6 Write an email to a friend. Write about what you've got in your bag. Ask about what your friend has got. Use your notes in Exercise 5 and the Focus box to help you.

5A

Vocabulary

Days of the week; everyday activities

1 Complete the words for days of the week.
1 S u n d a y
2 M _ _ _ _ _
3 _ r _ _ _ _
4 _ u _ _ _ _ _
5 _ h _ _ s _ _ _
6 S _ _ _ r _ _ _
7 W _ _ _ _ _ d _ _

2 Write the day of the week.
1 The day after Sunday.
   Monday
2 Day one of the weekend.

3 The day before Wednesday.

4 The day after Thursday.

5 Two days after Monday.

6 Day two of the weekend.

7 The day before Friday.

3 Complete the phrases with *have* or *go.*
1 ___*go*___ home at 6 o'clock.
2 _____ dinner in a restaurant.
3 _____ breakfast at 8 o'clock.
4 _____ to work every day.
5 _____ to bed at 10 o'clock.
6 _____ lunch at work.

4 Choose the correct alternatives.
1 We *get up* / *have* at 9 o'clock on Saturdays and Sundays.
2 I *go* / *watch* TV with my family.
3 I *work* / *study* in a cinema.
4 We *have* / *go* lunch at half past one.
5 They *go* / *have* to work at 8 o'clock.
6 I *go to* / *get* bed at half past ten.
7 We *study* / *get* at the university on Friday.
8 I *go* / *work* home at 6 o'clock.

Grammar

Present simple: *I/ you/ we/ they*

5 Choose the correct alternatives.
1 *I'm* / *I* go to work from Monday to Friday.
2 We *don't* / *no* watch TV on Saturdays.
3 We *not* / *don't* go to bed late.
4 On Mondays, they don't *have dinner* / *dinner* at home.
5 *They're* / *They* get up at 8 o'clock on Saturdays.
6 You *don't* / *aren't* work on Sundays.

6 Complete the sentences with the words in the box.

| at   from   on   to |

1 I work in a bookshop ___*on*___ Saturdays.
2 My children go to school _____ Monday to Friday.
3 _____ 1 o'clock, I have lunch.
4 I work from Monday _____ Wednesday.
5 We don't get up early _____ Saturdays or Sundays.
6 Sophie and Rosa go to bed _____ 10 o'clock.

7 Put the words in the correct order to make sentences.
1 dinner / with / have / I / on / family / Sundays / my
   I have dinner with my family on Sundays /
   On Sundays, I have dinner with my family.
2 on / have / lunch / don't / I / Tuesdays

3 don't / Fridays / I / on / Saturdays / work / or

4 Saturdays / to / 7.30 / study / We / from / on / 9.30

5 Saturdays / We / cinema / the / go / on / to

6 supermarket / Monday / work / Friday / to / I / a / from / in

Vocabulary
Travel and transport

1 Put the letters in the correct order to make travel and transport words.

1 toab ___boat___
2 ritan _____
3 lenap _____
4 xiat _____
5 cra _____
6 sub _____
7 kibe _____

2 Match the sentence halves.

1 I arrive ___e___
2 I ride my ____
3 On Mondays, I leave ____
4 My children travel ____
5 I drive to work ____
6 They don't cycle ____
7 I take ____
8 We don't ____

a in my car.
b to school by bus.
c bike to school.
d to work. They drive.
e at my office at 8 o'clock.
f home at 7.30.
g take the bus. We walk to work.
h a taxi from the station to my office.

3 Complete the description with words in the box.

arrive (x2) leave (x2) ride take travel walk

From Monday to Thursday, I get up at 5.30 and ¹ ___leave___ home at 6 o'clock. I ² _____ to the station and ³ _____ by train to London. I ⁴ _____ a bus from the station to my office. I ⁵ _____ at my office at 8 o'clock and have breakfast at my desk. I work from 8.30 to 5.30. I ⁶ _____ home at 7.30. On Fridays, I don't work. I get up late and don't ⁷ _____ home until 11 o'clock. I ⁸ _____ my bike to the supermarket and buy food.

Grammar
Present simple questions: *I/you/we/they*

4 Put the words in the correct order to make questions.

1 take / you / the / Do / work / to / bus ?
   Do you take the bus to work?
2 time / you / home / What / leave / do ?
3 office / How / travel / to / your / you / do ?
4 What / arrive / brothers / home / time / do / your ?
5 bike / school / you / your / ride / Do / to ?
6 friends / drive / university / your / to / Do ?
7 school / children / How / travel / do / your / to ?
8 supermarket / Do / you / your / walk / to / the / family / and ?

5 Match questions 1–8 in Exercise 4 with answers a–h.

___ a No, we don't. We drive.
___ b Yes, I do. I cycle every day.
_1_ c No, I don't. I travel to work by train.
___ d Yes, they do. They've all got cars.
___ e I take the bus.
___ f They walk.
___ g At 8 o'clock. I arrive at my office at 9 o'clock.
___ h At about 6 o'clock. We have dinner and watch TV.

6 Complete the conversations.

1 A: ___Do___ you travel by train to work?
   B: No, I _____ . I take the bus.
2 A: _____ your children cycle to school?
   B: Yes, they _____ .
3 A: _____ time _____ you get up?
   B: 9 o'clock.
4 A: _____ they drive to work?
   B: No, they _____ . They walk.
5 A: _____ you travel to work?
   B: I travel by boat.
6 A: _____ you and your friends take a taxi to the cinema?
   B: No, we _____ . We take the bus.

Vocabulary

Food and drink

1 Put the letters in the correct order to make words for the crossword.

Across
- 2 team
- 5 kecnhic
- 7 dabre
- 8 niwdsach
- 9 keac
- 10 gasru
- 11 offece
- 13 lasad

Down
- 1 sihf
- 2 kilm
- 3 eat
- 4 esehce
- 6 talehocco
- 12 gegs

2 Complete the table with the words from Exercise 1.

Food	Drinks
chicken	milk

3 Choose the correct alternatives.
1 I don't drink *coffee* / *bread* in the morning.
2 Do you put *sugar* / *cake* in your tea?
3 They don't eat *meat* / *milk*.
4 Do you put *milk* / *cheese* in your coffee?
5 We eat healthy food like *salad* / *chocolate*.
6 I don't *eat* / *drink* chicken.

Grammar

Present simple with frequency adverbs

4 Complete the sentences with the words in brackets.
1 I am late for work. (never)
   I am never late for work.
2 We have meat for dinner. (sometimes)

3 My children eat chocolate after lunch. (often)

4 I have a cup of coffee with breakfast. (always)

5 I cycle to work. (usually)

6 We eat healthy food. (often)

7 I have tea and cake in a restaurant. (sometimes)

8 We are at home for lunch on Sundays. (usually)

5 Correct the sentences.
1 I ~~sometimes am~~ late for work
   *I **am sometimes** late for work.*
2 How often you eat chocolate?

3 We eat usually lunch in a restaurant.

4 Always I have dinner with my family.

5 I go to bed late never.

6 We always are at home for dinner.

7 My friends buy usually sandwiches for lunch.

8 I eat often lunch at the office.

5D

English in action

Order food and a drink

1 Put the conversation in the correct order.

	a	How much is that?
	b	I'd like a black coffee please.
	c	Would you like sugar?
	d	Brown, please.
	e	I'd like a cheese sandwich, please.
	f	Would you like a drink?
1	g	What would you like to eat?
	h	Would you like brown or white bread?
	i	That's £7.20.
	j	No, thanks.

2 Complete the conversation with the words in the box.

cup   drink   egg   like   milk   much
that's   welcome   what   would

A: Hello, **1** .... would you like?

B: I'd like an **2** .... sandwich, please.

A: **3** .... you like brown bread or white?

B: White, please.

A: Would you like a **4** .... ?

B: I'd like a **5** .... of tea, please.

A: Would you like **6** .... ?

B: Yes, please.

A: Would you **7** .... sugar?

B: No, thank you.

A: OK, here you are.

B: How **8** .... is that?

A: **9** .... £7.80.

B: Thank you.

A: You're **10** ....

5

Listening

1 🔊 5.01 Listen to six people talk about how they travel to work. How many people travel by bus?

....

2 Listen again and write how many times you hear each type of transport.

car   *2*   bus   ....
boat   ....   taxi   ....
plane   ....   train   ....
bike   ....

3 Which types of transport do the people use? Complete the table.

	bike	car	taxi	bus	plane	boat	train	walk
1					✓			
2								
3								
4								
5								
6								

4 Complete the sentences with the words in the box.

always (x2)   never   often   sometimes   usually

Speaker 1
I ...*sometimes*... travel by train.

Speaker 2
I .... drive.

Speaker 3
I .... work at home.

Speaker 4
I .... travel by boat.

Speaker 5
I .... take the bus to college.

Speaker 6
I .... travel to work by train.

5

Reading

1 Read the article. What is Sally's job?

....

2 Match questions 1–7 with answers a–g in the text.

1 What do you have for dinner?   *f*
2 Do you work on Saturdays and Sundays? ....
3 What do you have for lunch? ....
4 Tell us about your day. What time do you usually get up? ....
5 How do you travel to work? ....
6 What do you have for breakfast? ....
7 Do you have lunch at work? ....

3 Are these sentences from Sally true (T) or false (F)?

1 I always get up early.   *F*
2 I always have a big breakfast. ....
3 I usually walk to work. ....
4 I have lunch at work. ....
5 I work from 9 to 5. ....
6 I sometimes have healthy food. ....
7 I have dinner in a restaurant on Thursdays. ....
8 I don't work on Thursday. ....

4 Match the words in the box with the meals.

| bread cake cheese chicken chocolate |
| coffee ~~eggs~~ fish green tea milk |
| salad sandwich tea water |

1 Breakfast: *eggs,*
....
....

2 Lunch: ....
....
....

3 Dinner: ....
....
....

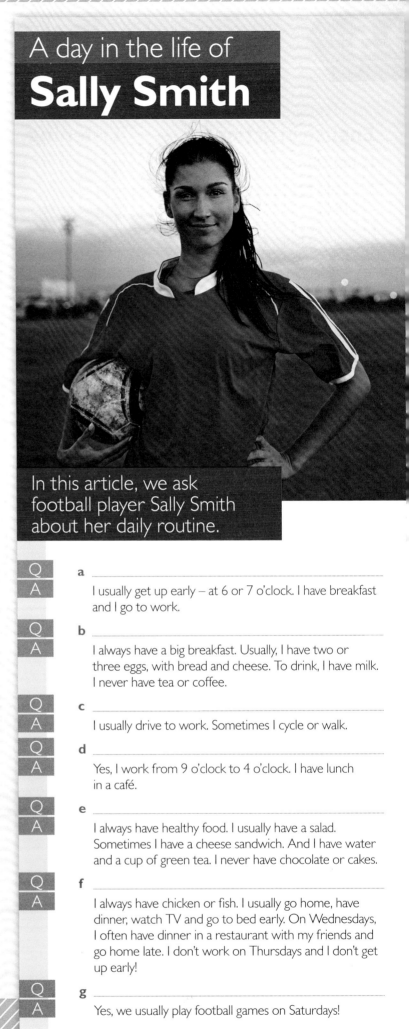

A day in the life of
Sally Smith

In this article, we ask football player Sally Smith about her daily routine.

Q a ....
A I usually get up early – at 6 or 7 o'clock. I have breakfast and I go to work.

Q b ....
A I always have a big breakfast. Usually, I have two or three eggs, with bread and cheese. To drink, I have milk. I never have tea or coffee.

Q c ....
A I usually drive to work. Sometimes I cycle or walk.

Q d ....
A Yes, I work from 9 o'clock to 4 o'clock. I have lunch in a café.

Q e ....
A I always have healthy food. I usually have a salad. Sometimes I have a cheese sandwich. And I have water and a cup of green tea. I never have chocolate or cakes.

Q f ....
A I always have chicken or fish. I usually go home, have dinner, watch TV and go to bed early. On Wednesdays, I often have dinner in a restaurant with my friends and go home late. I don't work on Thursdays and I don't get up early!

Q g ....
A Yes, we usually play football games on Saturdays!

5

Writing

1 Read the blog post. Are these sentences from Elena true (T) or false (F)?

A day in the life of
Elena Peters

I'm a doctor in a big hospital. I usually work from Monday to Friday, but I sometimes work on Saturdays and Sundays, too. I always get up at 7 o'clock. I have breakfast with my family and then I go to work at 8 o'clock. I usually cycle to work, but sometimes I take the bus. I never drive to work. I arrive at the hospital at 8.30. At 1 o'clock I have lunch. I often go to a café and I always have a cheese sandwich, a salad and a big cup of tea. The food is good, but the café is usually busy. I usually go home at 6.30, but sometimes I go to the gym first. At 8 o'clock I have dinner with my family. Then we often watch TV. I usually go to bed at 10 o'clock.

1 I never work on Saturdays or Sundays. _F_
2 I usually get up at 7 o'clock. ....
3 I sometimes take the bus to work. ....
4 I always have a sandwich and a salad for lunch. ....
5 I always go to the gym after work. ....
6 I usually go to bed at 11 o'clock. ....

2 Read the Focus box. Underline three adjectives and five adverbs of frequency in the blog post.

Using correct word order

	Subject	Verb	Object	Place/Time
	I	get up		at 7 o'clock.
	I	arrive		at the hospital at 8.30.
	I	go	home	at 6.30.
At 8 o'clock	I	have	dinner	with my family.

Put adjectives after *be*, but before nouns.
   The food **is good**.
   I have a **big cup** of tea.
Put frequency adverbs after *be*, but before other verbs.
   The café **is usually** busy.
   I **always get up** at 7 o'clock.

3 Rewrite the sentences using the words in brackets.
1 I am late for work. (never)
   I am never late for work.
2 I get up at 9 o'clock on Sundays. (usually)
   _____
3 I work from Monday to Friday. (always)
   _____
4 Has the café got food and drink? (cheap)
   _____
5 I take the train to work. (sometimes)
   _____
6 I work in a school. (small)
   _____

4 Put the words in the correct order to make sentences. Use capital letters and full stops or question marks.
1 usually / breakfast / at / have / I / o'clock / 8
   I usually have breakfast at 8 o'clock.
2 work / from / Do / always / Friday / you / Monday / to ?
   _____
3 usually / take / I / work / to / train / the
   _____
4 sometimes / go / café / I / for / to / lunch / a
   _____
5 I / TV / after / watch / never / dinner /
   _____
6 cycle / school / always / to / Do / you ?
   _____

Prepare

5 Make notes about your daily routine.

	When?	Notes
get up		
have breakfast		
go to work/school		
have lunch		
go home		
have dinner		
go to bed		

Write

6 Write a blog post about your daily routine. Use the blog post in Exercise 1, your notes from Exercise 5 and the Focus box to help you.

_____
_____
_____
_____
_____
_____

Vocabulary

Time expressions

1 Match the time expressions in the box with photos 1–6.

> at night at the weekend ~~every day~~ every week
> in the afternoon in the morning

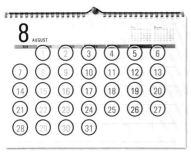

1 _every day_

2 _____

3 _____

4 _____

5 _____

6 _____

2 Choose the correct alternatives.

1 I usually study English _in the evening_ / in the morning after work.
2 My parents always get up at 8 o'clock _in the morning_ / in the afternoon.
3 We often have dinner in a restaurant _in the morning_ / at the weekend.
4 I usually go to bed at 11 o'clock _at night_ / in the evening.
5 I have a cheese sandwich for lunch _at night_ / every day.
6 They arrive home from school at 3 o'clock _in the afternoon_ / at night.
7 I talk to my parents _every week_ / every day – usually on Friday.
8 We don't work _every week_ / at the weekend. We work from Monday to Friday.

Grammar

Present simple: _he/she/it_

3 Rewrite the sentences to be positive or negative.

1 Alicia doesn't live in a small flat.
   Alicia **lives** in a small flat.
2 Max works in a big office.
   ....
3 Fred doesn't study English at the weekend.
   ....
4 Olivia doesn't watch TV in the evening.
   ....
5 Emily has eggs for breakfast.
   ....
6 Rafael goes to work at 8 o'clock.
   ....
7 Sophie doesn't finish work at 6 o'clock.
   ....
8 Henry eats lots of chocolate.
   ....

4 Correct the sentences.

1 My sister ~~live~~ in a small town in Mexico.
   My sister **lives** in a small town in Mexico.
2 Dan doesn't works at the weekend.
   ....
3 Beth don't wear glasses.
   ....
4 My housemate study English in the evening.
   ....
5 My parents goes to bed at 10 o'clock every day.
   ....
6 Paolo starts work at 9 and finish at 5.
   ....
7 I has a salad for lunch every day.
   ....
8 Sandy go to work at 6 o'clock in the morning.
   ....

5 Complete the text with the correct form of the verbs in brackets.

> My sister, Jane, **1** _lives_ (live) in Buenos Aires in
> Argentina. She **2** _____ (work) for a bank. She
> **3** _____ (get up) early and **4** _____ (leave) home at
> 6 o'clock. She **5** _____ (not have) breakfast at home. She
> **6** _____ (take) the train to work and **7** _____ (arrive)
> at her office at 6.30. She **8** _____ (start) work at 7 o'clock.
> She usually **9** _____ (have) lunch in a restaurant near
> her office. She **10** _____ (finish) work at 6 and
> **11** _____ (go) home. In the evening she often
> **12** _____ (have) dinner with friends. She
> **13** _____ (not watch) TV, but she often
> **14** _____ (study) Spanish and **15** _____ (read) books.

6B

Vocabulary

Jobs around the house

1 Cross out the word or phrase that doesn't match with the verb.

1 **clean**: the bathroom ~~the washing~~ the oven
2 **make**: the beds dinner the dishes
3 **feed**: the dog breakfast the children
4 **go to**: the washing the supermarket work
5 **cook**: dinner the kitchen lunch
6 **wash**: the beds the dishes the cups
7 **walk**: to the supermarket the dog the children
8 **do**: the washing the bathroom jobs around the house

2 Choose the correct alternatives.

1 I *cook* / *do* dinner for my family every day.
2 Jason never *does* / *goes* to the supermarket.
3 Our children never *wash* / *clean up* the living room.
4 Sara *makes* / *feeds* the dog in the morning and in the evening.
5 My brother and I *clean* / *do* the bathroom every week.
6 Jon always *washes* / *cleans up* the dishes after dinner.
7 I usually *clean* / *do* the washing at the weekend.
8 Rob *does* / *makes* his bed every morning.

3 Complete the sentences with the correct form of the verbs in Exercise 1.

1 I often ____*go*____ to the supermarket in the evening.
2 Jen never _____ her bed in the morning.
3 My sisters usually _____ their washing at the weekend.
4 My brother _____ lunch for us every Sunday.
5 Steve _____ the bathroom every week.
6 We _____ the dog every morning after breakfast.
7 Jo _____ the car every week.
8 Marion never _____ the dishes.

Grammar

Present simple questions: *he/she/it*

4 Complete the questions and answers with the correct form of the verbs in brackets.

1 A: *Does Ewa make her bed every day?* (Ewa / make)
   B: *No, she doesn't.* (✗)
2 A: Where _____ ? (Rebecca /live)
   B: In Paris.
3 A: _____ the dog? (he / walk)
   B: _____ (✗)
4 A: Who _____ in your house? (do the washing)
   B: My parents.
5 A: What _____ around the house? (Leo / do)
   B: He washes the dishes and cleans the kitchen.
6 A: How often _____ the kitchen? (Julia / clean)
   B: Every day.
7 A: _____ the bathroom? (she / clean)
   B: _____ (✓)
8 A: _____ dinner? (he / cook)
   B: _____ (✓)

5 Write present simple questions using the prompts.

1 How often / Beth / do / the washing?
   How often does Beth do the washing?
2 What jobs / Andy / do / around the house?
   _____
3 Mark / walk / the dog?
   _____
4 Who / wash / dishes / in your house?
   _____
5 When / the dog / have dinner?
   _____
6 Where / Peter / live?
   _____
7 Fatima / work / in an office?
   _____
8 How often / James / cook dinner?
   _____

6 Write questions for the answers.

1 A: *Where does Laura live?*
   B: Laura lives <u>in Madrid</u>.
2 A: _____
   B: She cleans the bathroom <u>every week</u>.
3 A: _____
   B: The train leaves at <u>3 o'clock</u>.
4 A: _____
   B: Yes, David <u>cooks dinner</u> every day.
5 A: _____
   B: Stef <u>cleans the kitchen and bathroom, washes the dishes and feeds the dog</u>.
6 A: _____
   B: No, Alex never <u>walks the dog</u>.

6c

Vocabulary

Skills

1 Complete the words and phrases.

1 bu**i**ld a w**e**b**s**i**te**
2 sw_m
3 r__e a h_r__
4 m_k_ a c__e
5 d_nc_
6 p_a_ f__t__l_
7 m__e cl____s
8 f__ a p__n_
9 s__ak t__ l_ng____s
10 s___p o_ a tr_i_
11 s_ng
12 d__w p_c_u_e_

2 Match the sentence halves.

1 Akira sometimes draws _c_
2 Claudia usually rides _____
3 Elena speaks _____
4 John always makes _____
5 My friends and I play _____
6 I build _____
7 Mehmet always sleeps _____
8 I don't make _____

a two languages.
b football on Saturday afternoon.
c pictures at the weekend.
d websites for my job.
e horses at the weekend.
f clothes for my children.
g on the train.
h a cake for my birthday.

3 Complete the sentences with verbs in Exercise 1.

1 I cook dinner for my family, but I never _make_ cakes.
2 Jon usually _____ at the swimming pool on Friday.
3 My dad sometimes _____ planes at the weekend.
4 Kate _____ two languages – English and French.
5 On Wednesday, we usually _____ football.
6 I sometimes _____ on the train after work.
7 At the weekend, we always go to a club and _____ .
8 George often _____ clothes for a shop in town.

Grammar

can/can't for ability

4 Write sentences and questions using the prompts and can/can't.

1 Daniel / ride a bike, / but he / not ride / a horse.
   Daniel can ride a bike, but he can't ride a horse.
2 Leo / sing / and / dance / very well.
   ....
3 I / play the piano, / but I / not sing.
   ....
4 What / you / cook?
   ....
5 Chloe / make / cakes, / but she / not cook / very well.
   ....
6 How many / languages / Flora speak?
   ....

5 Complete the question and answers with the correct form of words in the box and can/can't.

build	cook	drive	make	play	ride	speak	use

1 A: _____Can_____ you _____ride_____ a bike?
   B: Yes, I _____can_____ . I cycle to work every day.
2 A: How many languages _____ Pedro _____ ?
   B: Two. He _____ Spanish and English.
3 A: _____ Charlie _____ a car?
   B: No, he _____ . He walks to work.
4 A: _____ you _____ clothes?
   B: Yes, I _____ clothes for my children.
5: A: _____ Alex _____ ?
   B: No, he _____ , but he _____ cakes.
6 A: Can Rosa _____ a computer?
   B: Yes, she _____ websites.

6 Write sentences about Paul and Katy using the information in the table.

	Paul	Katy
other languages	German	Spanish
ride a horse	✗	✓
fly a plane	✓	✗
cook	✓	✓
play football	✗	✓
dance	✓	✓

1 *Paul can speak German. Katy can speak Spanish.*
2 ....
3 ....
4 ....
5 ....
6 ....

6D

English in action

Make requests

1 Put the words in the correct order to make requests and answers.

1 please / I / computer, / can / your / use ?
Can I use your computer, please?

2 can / you / yes,

3 can't / you / sorry, / I'm

4 wash / can / the / you / dishes, / please ?

5 I / yes, / can

6 problem / no

2 Complete the table with the phrases from Exercise 1.

Making requests	Saying yes to requests	Saying no to requests
Can I use your computer, please?	Sure.	I'm sorry, I can't.

3 Complete the requests and answers with words from Exercises 1 and 2 and the verbs in the box.

~~do~~   help   play   use   walk   wash

1 A: _____*Can you do*_____ the washing, please?
 B: _____*Sure*_____ ! They're my clothes!

2: A: _____ your phone?
 B: Yes, _____ . It's in my bag.

3: A: _____ the dog, please?
 B: I'm sorry, _____ . I'm late for work.

4 A: _____ football with us on Saturday?
 B: _____, I can't. I work every Saturday.

5 A: _____ you?
 B: _____, you can. How much is this dress?

6 A: _____ the dishes please?
 B: _____ . And I can clean the kitchen, too.

6

Listening

1 🔊 6.01 Listen to the radio programme. How many people live in each house?

1 Erica's house _____
2 Will's house _____
3 Kelly's house _____

2 Listen again and choose the correct alternatives.

1 *Erica / Erica's husband* always cooks.
2 *Erica / Erica's husband* cleans the bathroom.
3 *Erica / Erica's children* feed(s) the dog.
4 *Will / Will's wife* cooks dinner.
5 *Will / Will's wife* cleans the kitchen.
6 *Will / Will's wife* makes the beds.
7 *Kelly / Kelly's sister* always cooks.
8 *Kelly / Kelly's sister* cleans the bathroom.

3 Listen again. What jobs do the people do in the house?

1 Erica   *cleans the bathroom,*

2 Erica's husband

3 Erica's children

4 Will

5 Will's wife

6 Kelly

7 Kelly's sister

37

HELP Forum!

19 May at 11.32am

Sick of shared house living

I live with my best friend, Melissa. She's a great friend, but she isn't a great person to live with! I start work early every morning and I go to bed early. Melissa works for a music website. She works at home and doesn't get up early. Every night she watches TV and calls her friends. She always goes to bed late. And she isn't quiet! She sings and dances and I can't sleep.

She never does jobs around the house. I always clean up the living room and clean the bathroom. She can cook good food and she makes cakes, but she never cleans the kitchen or washes the dishes. Sometimes, she does the washing, but I usually do it. At the weekend, Melissa swims or goes to the cinema or has lunch in a restaurant. I always go to the supermarket and buy food!

We've got a dog, Perrito, but Melissa never walks him or feeds him! Sometimes I ask her to walk the dog, but she always says she can't.

What can I do? Melissa's my friend, but I can't live with her!

Lara

Reading

1 Read the forum post. Choose the correct alternative.

Melissa *works / lives / studies* with Lara.

2 Read the post again. Are the sentences true (T) or false (F)? Correct the false sentences.

1 Melissa is a great person to live with. *F*
 Melissa is a great friend, but she isn't a great person to live with.

2 Lara goes to bed early every night. ....

3 Melissa works in an office. ....

4 Melissa sends emails every night. ....

5 Melissa can't cook or make cakes. ....

6 Lara always goes to the supermarket at the weekend. ....

7 Melissa and Lara have got a cat. ....

8 Lara says she can't live with Melissa. ....

3 Complete the sentences with *Melissa* or *Lara*.

1 ____*Lara*____ starts work early every day.

2 _____ works for a music website.

3 _____ never cleans the bathroom.

4 _____ usually does the washing.

5 _____ goes to the cinema at the weekend.

6 _____ never feeds the dog.

4 Complete words/phrases 1–8 with the words in the box. Read the post again to check.

call ~~clean~~ do feed go make wash work

1 ____*clean*____ the bathroom

2 _____ friends

3 _____ to the supermarket

4 _____ the dishes

5 _____ the dog

6 _____ the washing

7 _____ a cake

8 _____ at home

Writing

1 Read the blog entry and answer the questions.

Jobs around the house

I'm Abby. I live with my friends Alice and Eduardo. We all work in a school from Monday to Friday. Alice and I are teachers and Eduardo works in the school office. At 5 o'clock in the evening, we finish work and go home. Alice and I feed and walk our dog and Eduardo makes dinner at 6 o'clock. After dinner, I wash the dishes and Alice cleans the kitchen. We watch some TV and go to bed at half past 10 at night. At the weekend, we all do jobs around the house. On Saturdays, Eduardo cleans the floors, Alice cleans the bathroom and I clean the living room. I take the dog for a walk in the afternoon and Eduardo and Alice go to the supermarket. On Sunday mornings, we do the washing. In the afternoon, we make our lunches for the next week.

1 Where do Abby and her housemates work?

2 What time do they finish work?

3 What time does Eduardo make dinner?

4 Who washes the dishes after dinner?

5 What time do they go to bed?

6 What job around the house does Alice do on Saturdays?

7 When do Eduardo and Alice go to the supermarket?

8 When do they do the washing?

2 Complete the Focus box with the sentences in the box.

> At 5 o'clock in the evening, we finish work and go home.
> At the weekend, we all do jobs around the house.
> ~~Eduardo makes dinner at 6 o'clock.~~
> I take the dog for a walk in the afternoon.
> On Sunday mornings, we do the washing.
> We all work in a school from Monday to Friday.

Using time expressions

- At the start of a sentence:
  1
  2
  3
- At the end of a sentence:
  4 *Eduardo makes dinner at 6 o'clock.*
  5
  6

3 Complete the sentences with *in, on* or *at*.

1 I usually go to the supermarket _____ Monday evenings.

2 John is a taxi driver. He starts work at 9 o'clock _____ night.

3 Suzie cleans the bathroom _____ Saturdays.

4 James makes dinner _____ 7 o'clock every day.

5 I start work at 9 o'clock _____ the morning.

6 We clean the floors and windows _____ the weekend.

7 Kirsty takes the dog for a walk _____ the afternoon.

8 John has breakfast _____ 6 o'clock.

4 Correct the sentences.

1 From Monday on Saturday, Joseph works in a hospital.

2 Alison feeds the dog in 7 o'clock in the morning.

3 We always go to the supermarket in the weekend.

4 Jenny does the washing in Saturday mornings.

5 I usually go to bed at 12 o'clock in night.

6 On 8 o'clock, Alex always has breakfast.

Prepare

5 Make notes about jobs around your house. Who does them? When?

Write

6 Write a blog post about who does the jobs around your house and when. Use the Focus box and your notes from Exercise 5 to help you.

Vocabulary

Places

1 Put the letters in the correct order to make words about places. Then complete the crossword.

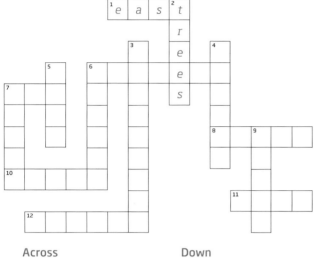

Across

1 seat ....
6 rowself ....
7 esa ....
8 hortn ....
10 lilsh ....
11 stew ....
12 dolucs ....

Down

2 sreet ....
3 tsnominua ....
4 dalins ....
5 alek ....
6 eldifs ....
7 houst ....
9 verir ....

2 Choose the odd word out.

1 river, lake, <u>sky</u>
2 north, sea, south
3 trees, river, flowers
4 island, mountains, clouds
5 sea, river, island
6 clouds, sky, lake
7 east, sky, west
8 fields, hills, trees

3 Complete the sentences.

1 There are lots of t*rees* .... in this park.
2 My family live in the s .... of Spain.
3 There aren't any c .... in the sky today.
4 There are red and yellow f .... in the field.
5 There's a big l .... in my town. People swim in it.
6 The name of the r .... in London is the Thames.
7 There are lots of m .... in Switzerland.
8 There's a small i .... in the lake.

Grammar

Wh- questions

4 Choose the correct alternatives.

1 *How much / How many* people live in your town?
2 *What / When* do you finish work?
3 *Who / How* do you spell your family name?
4 *How many / How much* is a sandwich and a cup of tea?
5 *When / What* is your birthday?
6 *What / Who* is the name of your city?
7 *Who / When* cooks dinner in your house?
8 *How much / How many* cars are there?
9 *Where / Who* is the hotel?

5 Correct six questions. Two questions are correct.

1 ~~How~~ do you live with?
   Who *do you live with?*
2 When does the train leave?
   ....
3 Who many trees are in the park?
   ....
4 How many is it?
   ....
5 How do you travel to work?
   ....
6 What do you spell the name of the hotel?
   ....
7 How much people do you live with?
   ....
8 What are you from?
   ....

6 Write questions using the prompts.

1 how / the red car?
   How much is the red car?
2 John / start work?
   ....
3 Greg / travel to school?
   ....
4 Amy's / birthday?
   ....
5 your / job?
   ....
6 do the washing / in your house?
   ....

7 Match questions 1–6 in Exercise 6 with answers a–f.

...... a My father usually does the washing.
...... b Her birthday is in May.
_1_ c It's £8,000.
...... d He starts at 9 o'clock.
...... e He usually rides his bike.
...... f I'm a nurse.

Vocabulary

Months, dates

1 Write the correct month.

1 The first month of the year.   *January*

2 The month before June.   _____

3 The month after February.   _____

4 Two months after September.   _____

5 The month after May.   _____

6 The month before May.   _____

7 The month after July.   _____

8 The month before March.   _____

2 Write the months in the correct order.

1 _____*January*_____   7 _____

2 _____   8 _____

3 _____   9 _____

4 _____   10 _____

5 _____   11 _____

6 _____   12 _____

3 Write the numbers.

1 fourth   *4th*

2 twelfth   _____

3 twenty-second   _____

4 first   _____

5 thirteenth   _____

6 eleventh   _____

7 thirtieth   _____

8 second   _____

9 fifth   _____

10 thirteenth   _____

4 Write the dates.

1 02/11   *the second of November*

2 19/05   _____

3 22/07   _____

4 29/01   _____

5 01/03   _____

6 16/06   _____

7 24/04   _____

8 11/12   _____

Grammar

was/were; there was/were

5 Rewrite the sentences in the past using *was*, *were*, *wasn't* or *weren't*.

1 It is Jack's birthday today.
It was Jack's birthday _____ yesterday.

2 The restaurant is busy tonight.
_____ last night.

3 We are on holiday this week.
_____ last week.

4 The hotel isn't quiet this month.
_____ last month.

5 There are ten people in my office this week.
_____ last week.

6 There aren't any people on the boat today.
_____ yesterday.

7 They are at the cinema today.
_____ yesterday.

8 You aren't at work this week.
_____ last week.

6 Correct the sentences.

1 It ~~were~~ my birthday last week.
*It **was** my birthday last week.*

2 The restaurant is quiet yesterday.
_____

3 There are lots of people at the party last night.
_____

4 Ali and I was at the cinema last Saturday.
_____

5 Esme isn't at work yesterday.
_____

6 The hotel were very expensive.
_____

7 The food were great at Lorna's party.
_____

8 My brothers are on holiday last month.
_____

7 Complete the text with *was*, *were*, *wasn't* or *weren't*.

> Last week I [1] _____*was*_____ on holiday in the south of Italy.
> I [2] _____ with my wife and children. We [3] _____ in
> a small town near a big lake. There [4] _____ mountains
> next to the lake and there [5] _____ a small island in the
> middle. There [6] _____ a boat to the island every day,
> but there [7] _____ (not) cars or buses on the island.
> Our hotel [8] _____ small and it [9] _____ (not) busy.
> There [10] _____ (not) a restaurant in the hotel, but there
> [11] _____ three in the town. One [12] _____
> expensive, but the other two [13] _____ cheap. The food
> [14] _____ great!

7c

Vocabulary
Adjectives

1 Write the opposite of each adjective. Use the words in the box.

difficult	fast	high	~~hot~~	long	light	old	sad

1 cold _____hot_____   5 happy _____
2 dark _____   6 low _____
3 easy _____   7 short _____
4 slow _____   8 young _____

2 Choose the correct alternatives.

1 My school holidays were _long_ / short. I was on holiday for seven weeks.
2 Jamie's building is low / _high_. It's got 30 floors.
3 My sister is five years old. She's old / _young_.
4 There aren't any mountains, but there are low / _short_ hills.
5 The bus is slow / _fast_. It takes four hours. The train takes two hours.
6 My English homework is very easy / _difficult_. I can't do it.
7 Wear a hat and coat! It's hot / _cold_.
8 I can't sleep. It isn't dark / _light_ in my bedroom.

3 Complete the sentences with the adjectives in the box.

dark	difficult	fast	happy	high	~~hot~~	long
young						

1 I never wear a coat in August. It's _____hot_____ .
2 That book is _____ . It's 600 pages.
3 Luca is _____ . He's on holiday for two weeks!
4 The mountains in my country are very _____ .
5 I can make clothes. It isn't _____ . It's easy!
6 The bus is slow. Take the train. It's very _____ .
7 I can't read my book. There aren't any lights. It's
   _____ .
8 My cat isn't _____ . It's 18 years old!

Grammar
was/were (questions), *there was/were* (questions)

4 Correct the conversations.

1 A: ~~Was~~ you on holiday last week?
   Were you on holiday last week?
   B: No, I wasn't.
2 A: The hotel was expensive?
   _____
   B: Yes, it was.
3 A: How much was your sandwich?
   B: It were £3.80.
   _____
4 A: Were Susan at home last night?
   _____
   B: Yes, she was.
5 A: Where Luke yesterday morning?
   _____
   B: He was at work.
6 A: Was there a party last night?
   B: No, there weren't.
   _____
7 A: Joanne and Katie were at school yesterday?
   _____
   B: No, they were at home.
8 A: How many people was at the meeting?
   _____
   B: About 20.

5 Complete the conversations with *was, were, wasn't* or *weren't*.

1 A: Where ___were___ you last night?
   B: I ___was___ at a party.
2 A: How _____ your holiday?
   B: It _____ great!
3 A: What _____ that book about?
   B: It _____ about football.
4 A: _____ the restaurant expensive?
   B: No, it _____ . It _____ cheap.
5 A: Where _____ Lyla and Leo yesterday afternoon?
   B: They _____ at the cinema.
6 A: _____ Sophie and Eva at the party?
   B: No, they _____ . They _____ at work.
7 A: How much _____ the hotel?
   B: It _____ £80 for one night.
8 A: _____ it cold last night?
   B: No, it _____ .

7D

English in action

Buy travel tickets

1 Put the conversation in the correct order.

.... **A:** Thank you. What platform is the train to Dublin, please?

.... **B:** Is that a single or return?

.... **A:** Thank you.

.... **B:** It arrives at 12.30. The fast train leaves at 10 o'clock and arrives at 12.15.

.... **A:** A return, please.

.... **B:** That's £62.50, please.

.... **A:** What time does it arrive in Dublin?

.... **B:** It leaves from platform 11.

.... **A:** OK. A ticket for the fast train, please.

.... **B:** The next train leaves at 9.20. It's a slow train.

_1_ **A:** Excuse me. What time is the next train to Dublin?

2 Complete the conversation. Write one word in each gap.

A: Can I help you?

B: Two ¹ _tickets_ to Glasgow, please.

A: Is that single or ² ....

B: Single, please.

A: ³ .... 's £22.60, please.

B: Here you are. What ⁴ .... is the next train?

A: The next train ⁵ .... at 2 o'clock.

B: Thanks. What time does it ⁶ .... in Glasgow?

A: At 2.45. Here are your tickets.

B: Thank you. What ⁷ .... is the train to Glasgow, please?

A: It ⁸ .... from platform 5.

B: Thank you.

7

Listening

1 🔊 **7.01 Listen to the podcast about people's holidays. How many holidays were good?**

....

2 Listen again. Tick (✓) the adjectives you hear.

busy	☐	high	☐
cheap	☐	hot	☐
cold	☐	long	☐
dark	☐	low	☐
expensive	☐	old	☐
fast	☐	quiet	☐
good	✓	sad	☐
great	☐	short	☐
happy	☐	slow	☐

3 Complete the sentences with the names in the box.

Ben John Lisa Sara

1 _Sara_ was on holiday in November.

2 .... was on holiday with their parents.

3 .... was in Paris.

4 .... was on a busy train.

5 .... was near the sea.

6 .... was in a small town.

7 .... was on holiday in February.

8 .... was near museums.

4a Are the sentences true (T) or false (F)?

1 Lisa was on an island in the north of Thailand. _F_

2 The food was great in Thailand. ....

3 Ben's hotel was hot at night. ....

4 It was Ben's 40th birthday. ....

5 John was on holiday with his sister. ....

6 John's train was busy and slow. ....

7 Sara was in London for a weekend. ....

8 The restaurants in London were expensive. ....

b Listen again and check.

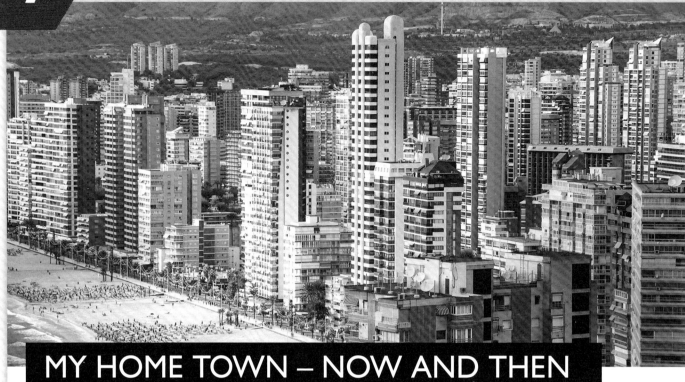

MY HOME TOWN – NOW AND THEN

My family is from a small island in the Mediterranean Sea. We live in a town in the east of the island. It's a big town – 50,000 people live here. Lots of people come here on holiday every year and in July and August it is very busy. There are lots of big hotels and high buildings. There are lots of cars and taxis. It is very hot in July and August – there's never a cloud in the sky! You can swim in the sea and walk in the mountains.

In 1930, when my grandmother was young, the town was very different – there were only 10,000 people here. Now you can fly here, but in 1930 there weren't any planes to the island. There were only slow boats. There were two boats every week. There weren't a lot of buildings and there were fields and trees around the town. There were no hotels and there was only one restaurant. There weren't lots of cars and taxis on the roads. In 1930, this was a quiet town and there were only Spanish people here. Now there are lots of people from different countries.

Reading

1 Read the article. Where is the town?

The town is _____ .

2 Read the article again. Answer the questions.

1 How many people live in the town now?
   _50,000_

2 When is it hot there?
   _____

3 What can you do there?
   _____

4 How many people were there in 1930?
   _____

5 How many boats to the island were there in 1930?
   _____

6 How many restaurants were there in 1930?
   _____

3 Choose the correct alternatives.

1 The town is in the _east_ / west of the island.

2 In July and August, the town is very busy / quiet.

3 There are lots of cars and taxis / buses there now.

4 There are / aren't any high buildings there now.

5 There were / weren't fast boats there in 1930.

6 In 1930, there were fields and flowers / trees around the town.

7 There were / weren't lots of hotels in 1930.

8 Now there are lots of people from Spain / different countries in the town.

4 Look at these adjectives. Write the opposite adjectives. Look at the article to help you.

1 fast	_slow_	4 low	_____
2 cold	_____	5 quiet	_____
3 old	_____	6 small	_____

Writing

1 Read the messages. Put sentences a–f in the correct order.

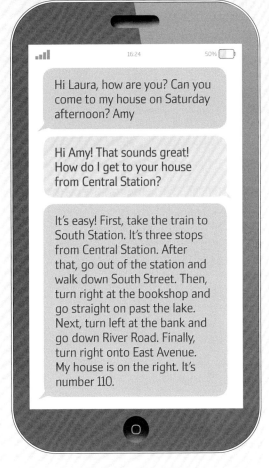

ᵃᵢₗ   16:24   50% 🔋

> Hi Laura, how are you? Can you come to my house on Saturday afternoon? Amy

> Hi Amy! That sounds great! How do I get to your house from Central Station?

> It's easy! First, take the train to South Station. It's three stops from Central Station. After that, go out of the station and walk down South Street. Then, turn right at the bookshop and go straight on past the lake. Next, turn left at the bank and go down River Road. Finally, turn right onto East Avenue. My house is on the right. It's number 110.

.... **a** Walk down South Street.
.... **b** Turn right onto East Avenue.
.... **c** Take the train to South Station.
.... **d** Go past the lake.
.... **e** Turn left at the bank.
.... **f** Turn right at the bookshop.

2 Read the Focus box. Complete the examples using the sequence adverbs.

Using sequence adverbs

Sequence adverbs are words like *first, then, next, after that, finally*. Use sequence adverbs to show the order you do something.

¹ _____*First*_____ , take the train to South Station.
² _____ , go out of the station.
³ _____ , turn right at the bookshop.
⁴ _____ , turn left at the bank.
⁵ _____ , turn right.

3 Complete the conversations with sequence adverbs.

1 **A:** Excuse me. Is there a bookshop near here?
   B: Yes. There's one on West Street. ¹_____ , you go down Park Street. ²_____ , you turn left at the cinema. ³_____ , go straight ahead past the university. ⁴_____ , turn right at the bank and walk next to the river. ⁵_____ , turn left onto River Road and the bookshop is on the right.
   A: Thank you.

2 **A:** Excuse me. Where's the Central Hotel, please?
   B: It's on Main Street. ⁶_____ , walk down Station Road to the bus station. ⁷_____ , take the 202 bus to the shopping centre. ⁸_____ , turn right onto Queen Street. ⁹_____ , walk past the university. ¹⁰_____ , turn left and the Central Hotel is on the right.
   A: Thank you.

Prepare

4 Read the notes and complete the table.

HOW TO GET HERE FROM LONDON

Blackwater Hotel

❶ 🚆 Waterloo Station – Southampton Central (1 hour 20 minutes)
❷ 🚶 Central Bus Station (5 minutes)
❸ 🚌 number 36 to boat terminal (7 minutes)
❹ ⛴ to West Cowes boat terminal (25 minutes)
❺ 🚶 to Quayside bus stop (3 minutes)
❻ 🚌 number 1 to Newport Bus Station (27 minutes)
❼ 🚕 to Blackwater Hotel (5 minutes)

Type of transport	From	To
Train		

Write

5 Write directions to the Blackwater Hotel from London. Use your notes from Exercise 4 and sequence adverbs.

_____
_____
_____
_____
_____
_____

Vocabulary

Verb phrases

1 Complete the sentences with the past simple form of the verbs in the brackets.

When she was young, Sally **1** _lived_ (live) in a big town. She **2** _____ (travel) to school every day on the bus and she **3** _____ (play) football with her friends every afternoon. She **4** _____ (love) football, but she **5** _____ (not like) tennis! Every Saturday, she **6** _____ (watch) a film at the cinema and then she **7** _____ (talk) about the film with her friends on the bus!

2 Match the sentence halves.

1 Every day, Tom travelled _____ _d_
2 Yesterday, I talked _____
3 Anna played _____
4 When Sarah was five, she lived _____
5 On Sundays, we travelled _____
6 When Jack was young, he loved _____

a tennis every Wednesday.
b in a village near Manchester.
c playing games on the computer.
d to work by train.
e about my weekend with my friends.
f to my grandparents' house for lunch.

3 Complete the sentences with a verb in the past simple form.

1 Simon _lived_ in the south of Spain when he was young.
2 I _____ to my friends about my favourite football team.
3 We _____ by train to Scotland every year.
4 They _____ all his films in one weekend!
5 The children _____ football on Saturday.
6 Jane and her sister _____ with their grandparents when they were children.

Grammar

Past simple (regular verbs)

4 Complete the sentences with the past simple form of the verbs in brackets.

1 I _visited_ (visit) my parents last weekend.
2 I _____ (not like) the food at my school.
3 We _____ (cycle) to school every day.
4 Louise _____ (not learn) another language at school.
5 Emily _____ (live) in Canada when she was 16.
6 I _____ (change) schools three times.
7 I _____ (not listen to) pop music when I was young.
8 We _____ (not watch) TV last night.

5 Correct six sentences. Two sentences are correct.

1 David ~~starts~~ work early yesterday.
   David **started** work early yesterday.
2 Ellie studyed English at university.
   _____
3 I didn't worked yesterday.
   _____
4 Jose didn't dance at the party last night.
   _____
5 Classes stoped at 3 o'clock at my school.
   _____
6 The train arrive late yesterday.
   _____
7 We played football on Saturday.
   _____
8 I no cleaned my house yesterday.
   _____

6 Rewrite the sentences using the past simple.

1 I don't travel to school by train.
   I didn't travel to school by train.
2 Fiona doesn't like the food in the restaurant.
   _____
3 Peter finishes work at 6 o'clock.
   _____
4 I talk to my brother on Sunday.
   _____
5 Jess doesn't clean the bathroom.
   _____
6 I study in the afternoon.
   _____
7 They walk to school every day.
   _____
8 I try new food on holiday.
   _____

Vocabulary

Irregular verbs

1 Complete the sentences with the verbs in the box.

> ate ~~bought~~ felt forgot got up met
> ran spoke

1 Tom __*bought*__ a new car last week.
2 I _____ at 8 o' clock in the morning.
3 We were late, so we _____ to school.
4 Yesterday, Anna _____ me in the coffee shop.
5 Tina lost her phone yesterday, so I _____ bad.
6 John and Frank _____ on the phone on Monday morning.
7 She _____ her bag at school on Friday.
8 We _____ really good food at the restaurant.

2 Complete the sentences with the past simple form of the verbs in brackets.

1 I __*met*__ (meet) my friend and we went shopping.
2 Jason _____ (not forget) his books on Monday.
3 They _____ (not take) the bus to work yesterday.
4 Jane feels bad because she _____ (lose) her phone last week.
5 My parents _____ (have) a really good holiday in Italy.
6 Linda and Alison _____ (go) to an expensive restaurant after work.
7 We _____ (not speak) on the phone yesterday.
8 Harry's new laptop _____ (break) on Monday.

3 Complete the sentences with past simple verbs.

> Yesterday, I **1** __*got up*__ at 8 o'clock and I **2** _____ breakfast. I **3** _____ to my friend Alan on the phone and I **4** _____ the bus to the park. I **5** _____ Alan there and we **6** _____ in the park for 1 hour. We **7** _____ to my house and we **8** _____ sandwiches for lunch. In the afternoon we **9** _____ to the shops and Alan **10** _____ a new phone. It was a great day.

Grammar

Past simple (irregular verbs)

4 Complete the crossword with the past simple of the verbs in the clues.

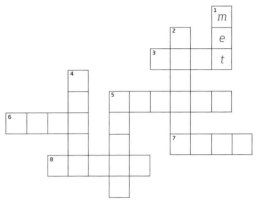

Across
3 lose
5 buy
6 feel
7 take
8 speak

Down
1 meet
2 forget
4 get up
5 break

5 Correct the sentences.

1 Yesterday, I ~~didn't gets~~ up early.
   __*Yesterday, I **didn't get** up early.*__
2 Rob's phone breaked yesterday.
3 Yuki didn't ate breakfast when she was young.
4 My sister goes to the cinema last night.
5 I didn't made a cake for my dad's birthday – my sister did.
6 Greg buyed a new computer last week.
7 Alison lose her money this morning.
8 I don't run in the park last Saturday.

6 Complete the text with the correct form of the verbs in brackets.

> I **1** __*had*__ (have) a great day yesterday! I **2** _____ (not go) to work and I **3** _____ (not get up) early. In the afternoon, I **4** _____ (go) to my friend's house and she **5** _____ (make) pizza for lunch. It **6** _____ (be) really good! In the evening, we **7** _____ (eat) really good food in a restaurant near the lake. I **8** _____ (forget) my wallet, but my friend **9** _____ (buy) dinner for me.

Vocabulary
Holiday activities

1 Choose the correct alternatives.

1 They *visit* / <u>*swim*</u> in the sea every morning.
2 Yesterday, we *went* / *had* shopping.
3 Last year we <u>*stayed*</u> / *visited* a small hotel.
4 They *have* / *go* for a walk in the mornings.
5 We *went* / *visited* to a restaurant with very nice food.
6 Tim and Anna always *have* / *go* a good time in Spain.
7 Sometimes, they *go* / *visit* museums in the city.
8 I *relaxed* / *visited* on my holiday last month.

2 Complete the sentences with the past simple or present simple form of the words in the box.

go	have	relax	stay	swim	visit

1 I *went* shopping yesterday and I bought a new book.
2 Every Saturday, they _____ a museum.
3 Tony _____ in the sea this morning.
4 My parents _____ to a restaurant every Sunday afternoon.
5 We _____ in the same hotel in Italy every year.
6 Yesterday, we _____ at the beach all day.
7 They _____ a good time at the party on Saturday.
8 Peter _____ for a walk yesterday.
9 Mark and Harry _____ three museums last week.
10 Jane and Sally _____ in an expensive hotel last year.

Grammar
Past simple (questions)

3 Complete the answers.

Did they have a good time at the party?

1 ____*Yes*____ , they did.

Did you have a nice holiday in the summer?

2 No, we _____ .

Did he have a good weekend?

3 _____ , he did.

Did you have lunch there?

4 Yes, I _____ .

Did she have dinner in a restaurant last night?

5 No, she _____ .

Did Peter have a nice party?

6 Yes, _____ .

Did they have breakfast with Sam?

7 No, _____ .

Did Tina have lunch with you?

8 _____ , she didn't.

4 Complete the questions with the words in the box.

How	What	When	Where

1 A: ____*How*____ did they go to school?
   B: By bus.
2 A: _____ did Maria and Jose go?
   B: To India.
3 A: _____ did he leave?
   B: Yesterday.
4 A: _____ did you travel to Italy?
   B: By boat.
5 A: _____ did you eat?
   B: Fish.
6 A: _____ did you do yesterday?
   B: We went to the beach.
7 A: _____ did Harry go?
   B: To the restaurant.
8 A: _____ did Sally do last week?
   B: She went on holiday.

5 Write questions using *Wh*- question words. Use the correct form of the verb in brackets.

1 *Where did you go on holiday last year* _____ ? (go)
   We went to Italy.
2 _____ ? (go)
   We went in the summer. It was very hot.
3 _____ with? (go)
   I went with my friend, Jenny.
4 _____ there? (travel)
   We travelled by bus and train.
5 _____ ? (see)
   We saw the Colosseum.
6 _____ ? (eat)
   We ate pizza and pasta.

English in action

Greet people

1 Choose the correct alternatives.

1 A: ¹*Bye / Hi* Rachel. ²*How / Who* are you?
 B: I'm ³*bad / good*, thanks. And you?
 A: I'm OK. How was your weekend?
 B: It was ⁴*great / thanks*! I went to a concert with my housemates and we had dinner in a restaurant.
 A: Did you like the concert?
 B: Yes, I did. I loved it. How was your weekend?
 A: It was ⁵*OK / well*. I went to the supermarket and cleaned my house.
 B: OK. Oh, here's my bus. ⁶*Bye / See* you later.
 A: Yes. See you.

2 A: Good ⁷*afternoon / later*, Gareth. How are you?
 B: I'm very ⁸*fine / well*, thank you. And you?
 A: I'm fine, ⁹*and you / thank you*. Did you have a good holiday?
 B: Yes, I did, thank you. It was very good.
 A: Where did you go?
 B: We went to the South of Italy.
 A: That sounds great! Oh, I've got a meeting now. Goodbye Gareth.
 B: ¹⁰*Goodbye / Hello* Alice.

2 Complete the table with the phrases in the box.

> Are you OK?   Bye.   ~~Goodbye.~~   Good afternoon.   Good evening.
> Good morning.   ~~Hello.~~   Hello. I'm good, thank you. And you?   Hi.
> How are things?   ~~How are you?~~   ~~I'm fine, thanks. And you?~~
> I'm great, thank you. And you?   I'm not bad, thank you. And you?
> I'm OK, thanks. And you?   See you.   See you later.
> Very well, thank you. And you?

Starting a conversation	*Hello.*
Questions for greetings	*How are you?*
Answers for greetings	*I'm fine, thanks. And you?*
Ending a conversation	*Goodbye.*

3 Complete the conversation with the words in the box.

> ~~are~~   bad   did   didn't   how   later   was   went

A: Hello, Martin.
B: Hi, Steve. How ¹ *are* things?
A: Not ² ____. And you?
B: I'm good! How ³ ____ your weekend?
A: It was OK. I worked on Saturday and on Sunday, I visited my parents. ⁴ ____ was your weekend?
B: It was great! I ⁵ ____ to Paris with my wife.
A: ⁶ ____ you take the train?
B: No, we ⁷ ____. We travelled by plane.
A: Great! Oh, here's my train. See you ⁸ ____, Martin!
B: OK, see you Steve!

Listening

1 🔊 8.01 Listen to a conversation between two friends. What do they talk about?
 a work   b the weekend   c holidays

2a Choose the correct option, a or b.

1 It's Zoe's ____ birthday at the weekend.
 a brother's   **(b)** sister's
2 Paul went to a ____ festival last year.
 a dance   b music
3 It was a ____ festival.
 a big   b small
4 Paul liked the ____ music.
 a Mexican   b Brazilian
5 Paul learnt ____ and Brazilian dances.
 a Mexican   b Turkish
6 The festival was ____ .
 a busy   b quiet
7 The food was ____ .
 a expensive   b cheap
8 Paul's friend ate ____ food.
 a Brazilian   b Thai

b Listen again and check.

3a Answer the questions.

1 Where is the festival?

2 How many countries are there dancers from?

3 What food did Paul eat?

4 What time did the festival finish?

5 Where do you get tickets for the festival?

b Listen again and check.

Reading

1 Read the story. Was it a good or bad day for Peter?

Peter usually got up at 6 a.m. because he started work at 8, but today was different. He got up at 10, and he had a slow breakfast at the kitchen table. He ate eggs and bread, and drank hot coffee. He didn't watch the TV, he didn't listen to the radio. It was quiet.

He usually took the bus with all the other people, or sometimes the car, but today he didn't take the bus and he didn't drive. He walked to the park. He met his friend. They usually ran in the park, but today Peter didn't want to run. They went for a walk, then his friend bought lunch. They spoke for a long time. Later, Peter went home and he sat in his garden. He listened to the birds.

Today Peter didn't break anything. He didn't forget a meeting. He didn't go to a busy restaurant. He didn't lose his phone on the bus. It was a good day.

2 Read the story again. Make a list of the regular past verbs and irregular past verbs.

Regular verbs
started

Irregular verbs
got up

3 Look at the photos and read the story again. Which things did Peter do? Which things didn't he do? Write a sentence for each photo.

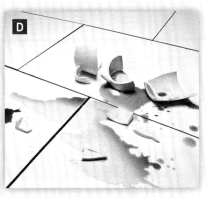

Writing

1a Look at the photos. Where do you think the places are?

b Read the text. Which place in Exercise 1a did the family go to on holiday?

My favourite holiday was in Spain in 2017. We went to Malaga. It's a small city in the south of Spain. We stayed there for two weeks. I went with my family – my parents, my brother Toni and my sister, Clara.

We stayed in a nice hotel near the sea. Every morning we went to a café for breakfast – the coffee was so good! Then, we went to the beach and relaxed.

On the last day, it rained so we went shopping. After breakfast, we took a bus to the shops and bought lots of things. In the afternoon, we visited the Picasso Museum. In the evening, we were tired and went to bed early!

It was a great holiday. We forgot our problems. After the holiday I felt sad. I often think about Malaga.

2a Read the Focus box. Then answer the questions in the box about the text in Exercise 1.

Planning your writing

Before you write a description of an event in the past, think about your answers to these questions:
- **What** was the event?
- **When** was it?
- **Where** was it?
- **Who** was there?
- **What** happened?
- **Why** was the event good/bad?
- **How** did people feel after the event?

Use times expressions and sequence adverbs to help describe the story:
In the morning, we took a train to Morocco.
Then, we walked in the park.
After lunch, we sang songs.

b Underline the time expressions in the text in Exercise 1.

3 Put the text in the correct order.

<u>_1_</u>   **a** We had a bad weekend last year in New York. On the first

_____   **b** We went to Little Italy for lunch, and we had a nice pizza. In the

_____   **c** we went to bed.

_____   **d** After breakfast we walked in the city, but the weather was really bad.

_____   **e** In the evening we were tired. We had dinner in the hotel, and then

_____   **f** day we had breakfast in the hotel. The food wasn't good.

_____   **g** afternoon we went to Macey's department store, but we didn't buy anything.

Prepare

4 You're going to write about a holiday you took. First, look at the questions and make notes.

- What was the event?

- When was it?

- Where was it?

- Who was there?

- What happened?

- Why was the event good/bad?

- How did people feel after the event?

Write

5 Write about your holiday. Use the notes you made in Exercise 4 to help you.

9A

Vocabulary

Prepositions of place

1 **Choose the correct option, a, b or c.**

1. **A:** Where's the cat?
   B: She's _____ the sofa.
   a between   b small   **c behind**

2. **A:** Where's your computer?
   B: It's _____ my desk.
   a at   b on   c between

3. **A:** Is there a bookshop near here?
   B: Yes, there's one _____ the park.
   a at   b by   c above

4. **A:** Who's that _____ you and your sister in the photo?
   B: It's my brother!
   a between   b on   c at

5. **A:** Where's Paul?
   B: He's _____ the train station.
   a above   b on   c at

6. **A:** Have you got a mirror?
   B: Yes, it's _____ the table.
   a above   b below   c at

7. **A:** Where are you in this photo?
   B: We are _____ Big Ben.
   a between   b on   c in front of

8. **A:** Where's Isobel?
   B: She's _____ her bedroom.
   a on   b in   c at

2 **Correct the sentences.**

1. There's a sofa ~~above~~ the bookcase and the table.
   *There's a sofa **between** the bookcase and the table.*

2. I worked in home on Thursday.
   ....

3. The train station is on front of the park.
   ....

4. We play football above the park every weekend.
   ....

5. I can't find my keys. I put them in the table, but they aren't there.
   ....
   ....

6. Can you clean up your bedroom, please? Your clothes are below the floor.
   ....
   ....

Grammar

Object pronouns (*me, him, her,* etc.)

3 **Match subject pronouns 1–7 with object pronouns a–g.**

1. she ———————— a them
2. I   b it
3. he   ——————— c her
4. we   d me
5. you   e us
6. they   f him
7. it   g you

4 **Choose the correct alternatives.**

> This is a photo of ¹*I / me* and my family. ²*We / Us* were on holiday in Paris. I'm between my mum and my sister. ³*She / He* is nine years old and ⁴*me / I* am 11. My brother is in front of ⁵*us / them*. ⁶*He / Him* is three years old. Behind ⁷*us / they* is the Eiffel Tower. ⁸*It / He* is very old. My dad isn't in the photo because ⁹*he / him* took ¹⁰*it / them*.

5 **Complete the conversations with the correct pronoun.**

1. **A:** Did you visit your family in Canada last summer?
   B: Yes, we visited _____*them*_____ in July.

2. **A:** Where does your brother live?
   B: _____ lives in Australia.

3. **A:** Can you take a photo of us?
   B: Sorry, _____ forgot my camera.

4. **A:** Can I visit you and Jess at the weekend?
   B: Yes, you can stay with _____ .

5. **A:** Did you call your sister last night?
   B: No, I didn't. I called _____ on Monday night.

6. **A:** I can't find my keys. Can you see _____ ?
   B: They're on the table.

7. **A:** What did you have for dinner last night?
   B: I had fish. I didn't like _____ .

8. **A:** How often do you walk your dog?
   B: I walk _____ every morning and evening.

Vocabulary

Hobbies

1 Complete the phrases with the verbs in the box.

> ~~do~~   listen to   play   read   use   watch

1. ___do___ some exercise / some sport
2. _____ a play / a TV programme / a film
3. _____ a story / a song / music
4. _____ a game / cards / a video game
5. _____ the internet / a computer
6. _____ a book / a newspaper / a story

2 Choose the correct alternatives.

1. I often *do / play* cards with my friends.
2. How often do you *read / watch* a newspaper?
3. We *watched / played* a great play at the theatre last night.
4. He *does / plays* some exercise every day.
5. Our children *listen to / play* stories every night.
6. Do you usually *watch / listen to* music in the morning?
7. I never *play / watch* TV at the weekend.
8. They *play / use* the internet every afternoon.

3 Complete the text with the correct form of verbs from Exercise 1.

> I usually **1** ___read___ a newspaper on the train to work or sometimes **2** _____ to a story on my phone. I don't usually **3** _____ books in the evening, but I do **4** _____ a lot of TV. Last night I **5** _____ a great film! My wife doesn't usually **6** _____ TV, but she **7** _____ the internet all the time! She always **8** _____ music and **9** _____ games on her computer. At the weekend, we **10** _____ some exercise together.

Grammar

like/enjoy/love/hate + -ing

4 Choose the correct alternatives.

1. **A:** Do you *like / liking* swimming?
   B: Yes, I *love / loving* it. I go to the pool every day.
2. **A:** What do you *like / don't like* doing at the weekend?
   B: I enjoy *go / going* to the cinema.
3. **A:** What does Dylan *likes / like* doing on Saturday?
   B: He likes *shopping / shop*.
4. **A:** What jobs do you hate *doing / do* around the house?
   B: I *hating / hate* cleaning the kitchen.
5. **A:** Does she like *listen to / listening to* music?
   B: Yes, she *love / loves* listening to music on her phone.
6. **A:** Do you like *travel / travelling* by plane?
   B: No, I *hate / am hating* flying. I never travel by plane.

5 Complete the text with the *-ing* form of the verbs.

> clean   cook   do (x2)   listen to   make (x2)   play
> read (x2)   watch (x2)

> I enjoy **1** ___watching___ films and I go to the cinema every weekend. I don't like **2** _____ TV programmes and I never watch TV at home. I love **3** _____ books and I read every evening before I go to bed. I like **4** _____ and I make dinner for my family every day. I don't like **5** _____ cakes, but my husband likes **6** _____ them. I love **7** _____ games with my children and **8** _____ stories to them. I think they enjoy **9** _____ my stories! I enjoy **10** _____ sport and at the weekend I always play tennis. I hate **11** _____ the bathroom and **12** _____ the washing.

6 Use the information in the table to write sentences.

	Emily	Oliver
draw pictures	✓✓	✗
watch TV	✓✓	✗
listen to music	✗	✓✓
play video games	✓	✗ ✗
swim	✗ ✗	✓✓
dance	✓✓	✓

1. *Emily loves drawing pictures.*
2. _____
3. _____
4. _____
5. _____
6. _____

9c

Vocabulary

Learning a language

1 Complete the missing letters to make phrases.

1 w _r i t_ e on the board
2 p _ _ _ an exam
3 m _ _ _ notes
4 d _ your homework
5 t _ _ _ an exam
6 r _ _ _ m _ _ r a word
7 u _ _ a dictionary
8 f _ _ _ an exam

2 Match the sentence halves.

1 We often go to   _c_
2 Last year, I took a   _____
3 Our teacher usually writes   _____
4 Can I use your   _____
5 Alison studies every evening so she always   _____
6 Did you do   _____
7 I always make   _____
8 I hate taking   _____

a passes her exams.
b exams. I never pass them!
c the library to study after class.
d cooking course. I learnt how to make bread and cakes.
e the answers on the board.
f notes in class.
g dictionary? I don't know how to say 'cheese' in Spanish.
h the homework last night? It was very difficult.

Grammar

why and *because*

3 Complete the conversations with the words in the box.

did (x3)   didn't   ~~do~~   haven't   is   were

1 **A:** Why _____ _do_ _____ you like studying English?
   B: Because I can talk to people from other countries.
2 **A:** Why _____ you go to Spain on holiday?
   B: Because my sister lives there.
3 **A:** Why _____ you do your homework last night?
   B: Because I went to the cinema.
4 **A:** Why _____ you fail the exam?
   B: I failed it because I didn't study.
5 **A:** Why _____ you got a dictionary?
   B: Because I use an app on my phone.
6 **A:** Why _____ you late for class?
   B: Because there weren't any buses this morning.
7 **A:** Why _____ you go to the library yesterday?
   B: Because I like studying there.
8 **A:** Why _____ English difficult for you?
   B: Because I can never remember words!

4 Match questions 1–6 with answers a–f.

1 Why do you like learning Spanish?   _f_
2 Why haven't you got a notebook?   _____
3 Why did you go to the library last night?   _____
4 Why did you get up early today?   _____
5 Why are you happy?   _____
6 Why are there no eggs?   _____

a Because I didn't go to the shop yesterday.
b Because I forgot it.
c Because I passed all of my exams.
d Because I wanted to study.
e Because I had an exam at 9 o'clock.
f Because I like listening to Spanish pop music.

5 Put the words in the correct order to make questions.

1 English / Why / you / studying / like / do ?
   Why do you like studying English?
2 is / library / in / Why / Carlos / the ?
   _____
3 got / pen / you / Why / a / haven't ?
   _____
4 didn't / study / Why / last night / you ?
   _____
5 sad / are / you / Why ?
   _____
6 did / Why / a / take / you / Japanese / course ?
   _____
7 John / Why / pass / the / didn't / exam ?
   _____
8 three / got / Marta / dictionaries / Why / has ?
   _____

English in action

Make and respond to suggestions

1 Match the sentence halves.

1 That's a	a like it.
2 When shall we	b something.
3 Sorry, I don't	c shall we go?
4 What shall	d great idea!
5 Good	e go at 8.30?
6 Let's do	f there last week.
7 Hmmm. I went	g idea!
8 Where	h go?
9 Shall we	i we play?

2 Complete the conversations with the phrases in the boxes.

> Good idea   I saw that last week   ~~Let's do something~~
> Shall we go   What shall we watch   When shall we go

1 A: **1** _Let's do something_ this evening.
   B: **2** .... What shall we do?
   A: **3** .... to the cinema?
   B: That's a great idea! **4** .... ?
   A: Let's watch *A Space Story*.
   B: Hmmm. **5** .... Let's watch *The City*.
   A: Good idea. **6** .... ?
   B: The film starts at 7.30. Shall we meet at 7 o'clock?

> I don't really like Mexican food   Let's go   Shall we go
> That's a great idea   When shall we go
> Where shall we go

2 A: Shall we have dinner in a restaurant tonight?
   B: Yes, **7** .... !
   A: **8** .... ?
   B: Let's go to that new Mexican restaurant.
   A: Sorry, **9** ....
   B: Really? I love Mexican food!
      10 .... to the Italian restaurant next to the cinema?
   A: Good idea. **11** .... ?
   B: Shall we go at 9 o'clock?
   A: That's late. **12** .... at 8 o'clock.
   B: OK.

Listening

1 🔊 **9.01 Listen to the podcast about learning English. Answer the questions.**
   1 How many people are learning English?
   2 How many people love taking exams?

2 Listen again. Are the sentences true (T) or false (F)?

Sofia
   1 She never passes exams. ....
   2 She loves watching TV programmes in English. ....
   3 She doesn't use apps for learning English. ....

Marta
   4 She never does her homework. ....
   5 She uses a dictionary on her phone. ....
   6 She likes reading books in English. ....

Onur
   7 He doesn't usually like studying. ....
   8 He took a two-week English course. ....
   9 He usually passes exams. ....

Guy
   10 He doesn't like speaking English to people. ....
   11 He likes doing his homework in the library. ....
   12 He uses the internet to watch films. ....

3a Write the names.

Who ...
   1 watches TV programmes in English?
      Sofia and ....
   2 never does homework? ....
   3 doesn't like studying? .... _and_ ....
   4 hates taking exams? ....
   5 reads newspapers in English? ....
   6 can't remember words in English? ....
   7 loves travelling? ....
   8 writes everything the teacher says? ....

b Listen again and check your answers.

Things I like!

Jim Robertson lives in Inverness in the north of Scotland, but he cycles all around the world. Last year he rode his bike 4,000 miles around the UK. He tells us why he loves cycling.

1 I started cycling in 2005 because I got a new job and started cycling to work. My office wasn't near my house and the bus was expensive, so I decided to cycle. At first it was difficult because I didn't do a lot of exercise and I wasn't fast. But I started to enjoy cycling to work and I started cycling at the weekend, too. Then, one summer I took my bike on holiday and cycled from the north to the south of Italy. It was a really good holiday and I loved cycling anywhere I wanted to go.

2 I love travelling and visiting new places. You can go places by bike that you can't visit by car or train. It's a cheap, clean and healthy type of transport. It's also quick. My cycle to work takes 20 minutes and the bus takes 30. I can stay in bed for an extra ten minutes each morning!

3 Nothing! I love everything about it.

Reading

1 Read the article quickly. What is it about?
a horse riding
b learning a new language
c cycling

2 Read the article again. Match paragraphs 1–3 with questions a–d. Write the questions in the article. There is one extra question you don't need.
a What don't you like about cycling? ....
b Why did you start cycling? ....
c How often do you cycle? ....
d Why do you like cycling? ....

3 Read the article again. Choose the correct alternatives.
1 Jim cycles *around the world / only cycles in the UK*.
2 He started cycling because he got a new *bike / job*.
3 When he started cycling, he was *slow / fast*.
4 One year he cycled from the *east to the west / the north to the south* of Italy.
5 He visits places you can't get to by car and *walking / train*.
6 Jim *doesn't love / loves everything* about cycling.

4 Read the article again and answer the questions.
1 How many miles did Jim ride around the UK last year?
....
2 Why did Jim start cycling to his office? (two reasons)
....
....
3 Why was cycling difficult at first?
....
4 Where does Jim love visiting?
....
5 How does Jim describe cycling? (four adjectives)
....
....
6 How long does it take Jim to cycle to work?
....

9

Writing

1 Read about Marta and Jan. Answer the questions with M (Marta) or J (Jan).

Marta

I like learning English because I love travelling and meeting new people. I can speak to people from all over the world in English. I usually watch British films and listen to music in English because I can learn lots of new words. But I don't like studying grammar because I think it's boring.

Jan

I like learning other languages because it's interesting and fun! I can speak English and Italian as well as Polish. I speak Italian every day because I work for an Italian company and some people in my office don't speak Polish. I speak English at home because my wife is British and she can't speak Polish.

Who ...?

1 thinks studying grammar is boring? _____
2 can speak three languages? _____
3 speaks English at home? _____
4 likes travelling and meeting new people? _____
5 watches British films? _____
6 works for an Italian company? _____

2 Read the Focus box and choose the correct alternatives.

Using *because*

Use *because* to give a reason.
I like learning English. Why?
I love travelling and meeting new people.
→ *I like learning English* **because** *I love travelling and meeting new people.*
I speak English at home. Why?
My wife can't speak Polish.
→ *I speak English at home* **because** *my wife can't speak Polish.*
I watch British films. Why?
I can learn lots of new words.
→ *I watch British films* **because** *I can learn lots of new words.*

1 We use *because* to answer the question *when?/why?*
2 We use *because* in the *middle/end* of a sentence.

3 Put the words in the correct order to make sentences.

1 reading / interesting / like / because / newspaper / the / I / it's
   I like reading the newspaper because it's interesting.
2 late / because / for / was / I / got / late / work / I / up
   _____
3 travelling / like / because / new / seeing / love / I / places / I
   _____
4 English / difficult / writing / don't / like / because / it's / in / I
   _____
5 because / I / to / love / the / every / cinema / go / week / films / I / watching
   _____
6 bus / the / I / to / because / drive / take / work / I / can't
   _____
7 like / don't / cleaning / house / the / I / boring / because / it's
   _____
8 yesterday / to / I / work / I / cut / my / didn't / hand / because / go
   _____

4 Use *because* to join 1–6 with a–f to make sentences.

1 I don't like living in the city
2 I like playing football
3 I never travel by plane
4 I ride my bike every weekend
5 I go to the market every week
6 I go to the theatre once a month

a I hate flying.
b it's my favourite sport.
c because I love shopping.
d I like watching plays.
e it's always busy.
f I love cycling.

1 *I don't like living in the city because it's always busy.*
2 _____
3 _____
4 _____
5 _____
6 _____

Prepare

5 Think of an activity you like doing. Why do you like doing it? Think of some reasons and make notes.

I like going to the cinema because I love watching films. I usually go with my best friend because she loves watching films, too.
_____
_____
_____
_____

Write

6 Write a short text about why you like doing the activity. Use the notes you made in Exercise 5 and the Focus box to help you.
_____
_____
_____
_____
_____
_____
_____

10A

Vocabulary

Collocations

1 Match verbs 1–10 with phrases a–j.

1	have	a	time with my family
2	try	b	jobs
3	join	c	a house
4	make	d	a business
5	change	e	to a big city
6	build	f	children
7	move	g	a new sport
8	start	h	some old clothes
9	spend	i	new friends
10	sell	j	a club

2 Choose the correct alternatives.

1 I didn't like my old job, so I *started* / *changed* jobs last year.
2 Last year, I *joined* / *built* a football team at work.
3 My parents *moved* / *built* this house in the 1970s.
4 I don't *make* / *spend* much time with my parents because I don't live near them.
5 My sister *had* / *tried* a daughter last year. Her name is Emily.
6 I *made* / *built* lots of friends when I was at university.
7 I went to a painting class last week because I wanted to *have* / *try* something different.
8 John *sold* / *moved* all his old books on the internet.
9 We're from a small village, but last year we *changed* / *moved* to a big city.
10 Florence loves making cakes and last year she *started* / *built* a small cake company.

3 Complete the text with verbs from Exercise 1.

I wasn't happy last year. I didn't like my job and I was always very busy at work, so I didn't [1] *spend* time with my family or friends. My flat was near my office, but it was very small, and I didn't like living there. In January, I decided to [2] _____ jobs and [3] _____ something different! I found a great job in a small town near the sea and I [4] _____ to a house near my new office. I didn't know anyone in the town, so I [5] _____ a running club. I [6] _____ lots of new friends and now I see them every week.

Grammar

would like/love to

4 Choose the correct option, a or b.

1 Where _____ you like to go this afternoon?
   a do   **(b)** would
2 I'd love _____ to a small village in the mountains.
   a to move   b moving
3 _____ to join a book club. I love reading.
   a I like   b I'd like
4 _____ you like to start a business?
   a Do   b Would
5 I _____ like to change jobs. I love my job!
   a don't   b wouldn't
6 I'd _____ to spend more time with my sister.
   a love   b loving
7 When would you like _____ on holiday?
   a go   b to go
8 Tom would _____ to try flying a plane!
   a loves   b love

5 Correct five more sentences. Two sentences are correct.

1 They ~~like~~ to have children in the future.
   *They **would like** to have children in the future.*
2 Jan would love start a clothes company.
   _____
3 A: Would you like to go to the party?
   B: No, I don't.
   _____
4 I'd like to change my old bike for a new one.
   _____
5 What do you like to watch at the cinema tonight?
   _____
6 I love my house, so I don't like to move.
   _____
7 Who would you like to sit next to?
   _____
8 James would like joining the gym.
   _____

6 Complete the questions with *would like* and the verbs in the box.

do	~~go~~	join	speak	study	watch

1 Where _____*would*_____ you _____*like to go*_____ on holiday?
2 A: _____ you _____ a film tonight?
   B: No, thanks. I've got lots of homework.
3 A: What _____ Sara _____ at college?
   B: Art. She loves painting and drawing.
4 A: What _____ you _____ in the future?
   B: I'd love to be a doctor.
5 A: What languages _____ you _____ ?
   B: Japanese and Arabic.
6 A: _____ you _____ a gym?
   B: Yes. I'd like to do more exercise.

Vocabulary

Party vocabulary

1 Put the letters in the correct order to make words.

1 gins _____sing_____
2 aslda _____
3 wandescsih _____
4 sirdkn _____
5 ankscs _____
6 tresesd _____
7 cenda _____
8 klat _____
9 itnels _____
10 uritf _____
11 yalp _____

2 Match the sentence halves.

1 My dad often sings _____d_____
2 Anna loves to listen _____
3 Me and my friends play _____
4 Every day, I talk _____
5 We always like to _____

a to friends at school.
b to songs on her phone.
c dance at parties.
d songs in the bathroom.
e games every Saturday.

Grammar

be going to

3 Put the words in the correct order to make sentences.

1 my / visit / I'm / parents / to / going
   I'm going to visit my parents.
2 Lucia / my house / to / is / going / come / to
   _____
3 a / are / going / watch / We / film / to
   _____
4 football / not / are / play / They / to / going
   _____
5 going / be / restaurant / a / is / The party / at / to
   _____
6 She / arrive / to / 8 o'clock / the / going / is / at
   _____
7 move / going / to / house / I'm / new / a / to
   _____
8 going / Edward / to / isn't / school / go / to
   _____

4 Correct the sentences.

1 I going to study French next year.
   I'm going to study French next year.
2 My brother's going change jobs next month.
   _____
3 Charlotte and Leonie is going to visit the museum.
   _____
4 I'm not going doing anything on Saturday!
   _____
5 They aren't going take the train to Paris.
   _____
6 We isn't going to play the game.
   _____
7 I go to have dinner with Martin tomorrow.
   _____
8 Jenny going to have a baby next year.
   _____

5 Complete the sentences with *be going to* and the verbs in brackets.

1 I _____'m going to see_____ (see) Tim at the weekend.
2 We _____ (not go) on holiday this year.
3 Luisa _____ (open) an Italian restaurant.
4 My parents _____ (sell) their house.
5 Sam _____ (change) jobs.
6 Frank _____ (not move) to the city next year.
7 You _____ (play) the game!
8 I _____ (not dance) at the party.

Vocabulary

Seasons; time expressions

1 Complete the months.

1 J a n u a r y
2 F _ _ _ _ a _ _
3 M _ _ _ _
4 A _ _ _ _
5 M _ _
6 J _ _ _
7 J _ _ _
8 A _ _ _ s _
9 S _ _ _ e _ _ _ _
10 O _ _ _ _ _ _ r
11 N _ _ _ m _ _ _
12 D _ _ e _ _ _ _

2 Complete the text with the items in the box.

in	for (x2)	fortnight	on	st
~~summer~~	th	winter	with	

In the **1** _summer_ , we are going to travel to Spain. We're going to stay for a **2** _____ because we always go **3** _____ two weeks. We are going **4** _____ August and we are going to stay **5** _____ my grandparents. We are going to travel **6** _____ 2nd August and we leave Spain on the 16 **7** _____ . We love visiting our grandparents and every **8** _____ they travel to London and stay with us **9** _____ six weeks. They usually travel on 1 **10** _____ December. They're great!

Grammar

be going to: questions

3 Choose the correct alternatives.

1 **A:** *Are you / You are* going to do your homework this afternoon?
   B: No, *I'm not / I aren't*. I'm going to do it tomorrow.
2 **A:** *Are we / Is we* going to visit Stephen this month?
   B: Yes, *we are / we're*.
3 **A:** What are you going *watch / to watch* at the cinema?
   B: *We're / We* going to watch *Summer Story*.
4 **A:** *Does / Is* she going to start dance classes?
   B: No, she *isn't / not*.
5 **A:** When *is / are* they going to arrive?
   B: They *are / is* going to arrive in August.
6 **A:** Where *are / is* you going to go on holiday this year?
   B: *I / I'm* going to visit my sister in Argentina.

4 Write questions with *be going to* using the prompts.

1 you / study / history / at university / next year?
   Are you going to study history at university next year?
2 you / move / to another city / next year?
   _____
3 Duncan / play / football / tomorrow?
   _____
4 Emma and George / visit / us / this weekend?
   _____
5 we / late / for class?
   _____
6 they / learn / Spanish?
   _____
7 Alex / make dinner / tonight?
   _____
8 you / take / train / to London?
   _____

5 Complete the short answers.

a No, _we're not_ . We're going to take the plane.
b No, _____ . We're going to be on time.
c Yes, _____ . They're going to play games.
d Yes, _____ . She's going to make pizza.
e No, _____ . He's playing tennis.
f No, _____ . I'm going to study English and French.
g Yes, _____ . They're going to arrive on Saturday.
h Yes, _____ . I'm going to move to Buenos Aires.

6 Match answers a–h with questions 1–8 in Exercise 4.

1 ____ 2 ____ 3 ____ 4 ____
5 ____ 6 ____ 7 ____ 8 ____

English in action

Make and respond to invitations

1 Complete the conversation with phrases a–d.

A: Hi Nadya, how are you?

B: Not bad, thanks. And you?

A: Great thanks. Listen, I'm going to have dinner with Jess next week. **1** _____ .

B: **2** _____ .

A: OK, another time.

B: But, have you got plans for tomorrow night? There's a good film on at the cinema – *Fire Mountain*. I'm going to get tickets. **3** _____ .

A: **4** _____ . What time does the film start?

B: At 8.15. Shall we meet at the cinema at 8 o'clock?

A: That sounds good.

B: Great! See you tomorrow.

A: Yeah, see you tomorrow.

a Sorry, I can't because I'm going to have dinner with Ben.

b I'd love to, thanks.

c Would you like to come with us?

d Would you like to come with me?

2 Match invitations 1–6 with responses a–f.

1 We're going to have a party at our flat. Would you like to come? _____

2 Dan and I are going to have lunch on Sunday. Would you like to join us? _____

3 We're going to watch the football game tomorrow. Would you like to come? _____

4 I'm going to do my homework in the library this afternoon. Would you like to come with me? _____

5 Would you like to come to the theatre with me next week? I'm going to see a play in Spanish. _____

6 We're going to have a picnic in the park on Friday. Would you like to have lunch with us? _____

a I'd love to! But I think it's going to rain on Friday.

b That would be great! Shall we meet at the library after lunch?

c Sorry, I can't because I work on Sundays.

d Thanks, but I don't really like watching sport.

e I'd love to! Where do you live?

f Thanks, but I can't speak Spanish!

Listening

1 ◀)) 10.01 Listen to two friends talk about what they're going to do when they finish school. What jobs would they like to do in the future?

Jack _____   Sabrina _____

2 Listen again. Put the questions in the order you hear them.

a Which places are you going to visit in India? _____

b Who are you going to go with? _____

c What are you going to do next year, Jack? _____

d What are you going to do after your trip to India? _____

e How long are you going to go for? _____

f Are you going to go to university? _____

3 Listen again. Write Sabrina (S), Jack (J) or both (S/J).

1 _____ is going to travel to India.

2 _____ would like to visit the Taj Mahal.

3 _____ loves taking photographs.

4 _____ is going to study English.

5 _____ is going to study in Birmingham.

6 _____ would like to go to Italy.

4 Choose the correct option, a or b.

1 Who is Jack going to go to India with?
   a friends from his football club
   b friends from school

2 Which part of India is Jack going to visit?
   a the sea   b the mountains

3 Where is Jack going to study art?
   a university   b college

4 When is Sabrina going to move to Birmingham?
   a in the summer   b in the autumn

5 Where is Sabrina going to work in the summer?
   a a bookshop   b a supermarket

6 Why does Sabrina want to go to Italy?
   a She loves Italian music.   b She loves Italian food.

5 Listen again and check.

Reading

1 Read the introduction to the article. What type of business did Amy start?

_____

Amy Hughes started a clothes
company after she had her first
child in 2014. Now, she's got two
shops and sells clothes on the
internet to people all over the world.
Here she tells us about her dreams
for the future.

'After I had my daughter in 2014, I wanted
to change jobs. I was a teacher and I loved
my job, but I was very busy at work and I
didn't spend a lot of time with my family
and friends. I loved making clothes and
I made lots of clothes for my daughter.
I started a small company and sold clothes on
the internet. Now I've got two small shops!

Next year, I'm going to open another shop.
Now, I only sell children's clothes, but I'm
going to sell clothes for women, too. In the
future, I'd like to make shoes. And I'd love to
open a big shop in London.

I really love my job, but I'm very busy. In the
future, I'm not going to work at weekends or
in the school holidays. I'd really like to travel
to lots of different places. I'd also like to join
a gym and do more exercise! And I'd really
love to move to a big house by the sea!'

2 Read the rest of the article and put the topics in the correct order.
a Amy's future plans for her company _____
b Amy's future plans for herself _____
c why she started a business _____

3 Read the article again. Are the sentences true (T) or false (F)?
Correct the false sentences.
1 Amy Hughes has got three clothes shops. _____
_____
2 She liked being a teacher. _____
_____
3 Now she sells clothes for women and children. _____
_____
4 In the future, she'd like to make bags. _____
_____
5 In the future, she's not going to work in the school holidays. _____
_____
6 She'd like to join a book club and read more books. _____
_____

4 Answer the questions.
1 When did Amy start her business?
_____
2 Why did Amy want to change jobs?
_____
3 When is Amy going to open
another shop?
_____
4 Where would Amy like to open a
big shop?
_____
5 Where would Amy like to travel to?
_____
6 Where would Amy like to move to?
_____

10

Writing

1 Read the messages. Which two people's summer activities do the photos show?

Summer holidays

4 posts

Elif — Hi everyone! What are your plans for the summer holidays? I'm going to visit my brother in Canada. He lives in Vancouver. I'm going to stay with him for three weeks.

Josie — That sounds great! I'm going to work in the summer. I've got a job in a café. It's next to the lake.

Sophie — I'm going to go to Japan with my flatmates. They're in Japan now. I'm going to meet them in Tokyo next week and travel around with them for two weeks.

Marco — I'm going to work with my parents. They've got an Italian restaurant in the town centre and I'm going to help them cook.

2 Read the messages again and complete the sentences.
1 _____ is going to work in his parents' restaurant.
2 _____ is going to Japan with her flatmates.
3 _____ is going to work in a café.
4 _____ is going to stay with her brother in Canada.

3 Read the Focus box. Choose the correct pronouns.

Using subject and object pronouns

Don't write the same names a lot. Use:
• subject pronouns: *I, you, he, she, it, we, you, they*
• object pronouns: *me, you, him, her, it, us, them.*
I'm going to visit my brother in Canada.
~~My brother~~ **He** lives in Vancouver. I'm going to stay with ~~my brother~~ **him** for three weeks.
I'm going to go to Japan with my flatmates. ¹*You/They* are in Japan now. I'm going to meet ²*us/them* in Tokyo next week and travel around with ³*him/them* for two weeks.

4 Complete the sentences with subject or object pronouns.
1 I tried Japanese food last week and I loved ____*it*____ .
2 I'm going to stay with my parents in the summer. _____ live next to a big lake.
3 Fiona and I are going to see our brother next week. He's going to stay with _____ .
4 My sister loves music. _____ always goes to concerts.
5 My friend, David, lives in Hong Kong. I'm going to visit _____ in the summer.
6 I've got lots of American films. I love watching _____ .

5 Correct the sentences.
1 In the summer holidays, I'm going to go to Italy with my friend. ~~They~~ are going to take the boat.
... ***We*** *are going to take the boat.*
2 I can't speak Spanish, but I'm going to study her next year.
_____
3 Dan loves music, but she can't sing!
_____
4 My parents live in New York. I'm going to visit us next year.
_____
5 Jane and I lived together for two years. They had a flat in the centre of Madrid.
_____
6 Sam made pizza last night. She was great!
_____

6 Choose the correct alternatives.

In the summer holidays, I'm going to do lots of things. First, I'm going to work in a restaurant. ¹*It / He* is a small Thai restaurant near my house. Then, I'm going to visit my parents. ²*They / You* live in London. I'm going to stay with ³*them / they* for three days. Then I'm going to travel to Spain to see my sister. ⁴*She / Her* lives in Barcelona. I'm going to stay with ⁵*her / him* for two weeks and ⁶*we / us* are going to visit interesting places and go to the beach.

Prepare

7 Make notes about what you're going to do next summer. What? Where? Who with?
I'm going to visit my friends in Cambridge. We're going to take a boat on the river.
_____
_____
_____

Write

8 Write a message for an online discussion about your plans for the summer. Use your notes from Exercise 7 and the Focus box to help you.
_____
_____
_____
_____
_____

AUDIO SCRIPTS

UNIT 1   Recording 1

1

L = Lucia   G = Gosia

L: Hi, I'm Lucia. What's your name?

G: Hi, I'm Gosia. Nice to meet you.

L: Nice to meet you too. Where are you from?

G: I'm from Poland.

L: My friend Laura is Polish too, but she isn't in this class. Are you from Warsaw?

G: No, I'm from Poznan. Where are you from?

L: I'm from Argentina. I'm a student at a university in Buenos Aires. Are you a student, too?

G: No, I'm an office worker. Is this your first time in the UK?

L: Yes, it is. Is it your first time, too?

G: Yes! I'm very happy to be here. Who's that?

L: That's Jane. She's the teacher. She's from Canada.

2

M = Maria   D = David   S = Sarah

M: Hi, I'm Maria.

D: Hi Maria, I'm David and this is Sarah. Is this your first day?

M: Yes, it is. I'm a student nurse.

S: We're students, too. I'm a student doctor and David's a student nurse. Where are you from Maria?

M: I'm from Brazil.

D: I'm Brazilian, too! I'm from Rio. Where are you from?

M: I'm from São Paolo. Where are you from Sarah?

S: I'm from Manchester in the UK.

3

C = Cristina   P = Pete

C: Hello, I'm Cristina Sanchez. Nice to meet you.

P: Hello, I'm Pete Capaldi. Nice to meet you.

C: Where are you from Pete?

P: I'm from the UK. I'm from London. Where are you from?

C: I'm from Spain. Are you a speaker at the conference?

P: Yes, I am.

C: Are you a teacher?

P: Yes, I am. I work in a big university in London. Are you a teacher, too?

C: No, I'm not. I'm a manager at a language school in Madrid.

UNIT 2   Recording 1

I = Interviewer   M = Maija   K = Kevin   A = Amelia

I: Hello and welcome to *London Life*. Today we're in Covent Garden to ask people '*what's in your bag?*' Excuse me. Can I ask you some questions? It's for a podcast.

M OK.

I: What's your name?

M: Maija.

I: Where are you from, Maija?

M: I'm from Poland.

I: And what's in your bag?

M: My bag? My phone, my keys, my credit card and a book.

I: Thank you very much.

I: Hello, excuse me!

K: Can I help you?

I: Yes! Can I ask you some questions for a podcast?

K: Yeah, sure.

I: First, what's your name?

K: It's Kevin.

I: And where are you from?

K: I'm from London.

I: And what's in your bag today?

K: A book, my computer, … keys, cash. I think that's all.

I: Thanks very much, Kevin.

I: Hi, can I ask you some questions?

A: Some questions? Why?

I: It's for a podcast.

A: Oh, OK.

I: What's your name?

A: It's Amelia.

I: And where are you from?

A: I'm from Vancouver, Canada.

I: And what's in your bag, Amelia?

A: Let's see … my phone, my passport, my camera, cash. And photos of my family.

I: Great, thanks Amelia!

UNIT 3   Recording 1

1

My town is great! It isn't big, but there are lots of restaurants and cafés. There's a good Turkish restaurant and a new Mexican restaurant … and there's a Japanese restaurant next to the Turkish one, but it's expensive. There's a big cinema and a good bookshop … and there's a big park next to the school.

2

My town is very small. There aren't any restaurants, but there are two cheap cafés. … There aren't any supermarkets, but there's a market on Main Street. There's a small school and an old cinema. There isn't a train station and there aren't any hotels. It's a very quiet town!

3

My town is big. There are lots of flats and big offices. There's a big train station, a university and a hospital. There are four supermarkets and a market. There's a good Spanish restaurant and a great Turkish café. There are hotels and cinemas. There aren't any big parks, but there are two small parks. It's a busy town!

UNIT 4 Recording 1

L = Leo   S = Sarah

L: Hello? Hello? Sarah?

S: Hi, hi Leo. Are you with Uncle Joe?

L: No, your Uncle Joe is not here!

S: He is!

L: He's not here ... Oh, wait – has he got a beard?

S: Yes, do you see him?

L: Has he got blue eyes?

S: Yes. Very blue.

L: Is he about 50 years old?

S: Yes. Leo, say hello to him now ...

L: And has he got blonde hair?

S: Blonde? No, his hair isn't blonde. Leo, it's brown. He has usually got a black coat on.

L: Oh. OK. That's not your Uncle Joe.

S: Leo, where are you?

L: I'm at the airport.

S: Leo. My uncle is at the hotel. The Plaza hotel, Leo. Leo?

UNIT 5 Recording 1

1

I travel by plane to work! My house is in Paris and my job is in London. I take the plane to London on Mondays and go home to Paris on Thursdays. I sometimes travel by train, but usually I take the plane.

2

My flat is near my office, so I always ride my bike or walk to work. I haven't got a car, so I never drive.

3

I usually work at home, so I don't usually travel to work. I sometimes take the bus or a taxi to my office.

4

I often travel by boat to my office, but sometimes I take the train. My house isn't near my office. I get up at 6, leave home at 7 and arrive at work at 8.

5

I always take the bus to college. My house is near the college, so I leave home at 8 o'clock, take the bus and arrive at college at 8.30.

6

I haven't got a car, so I always travel to work by train. I take a taxi or the bus from the train station to my office.

UNIT 6 Recording 1

M = Mike   E = Erica   W = Will   K = Kelly

M: Good morning and welcome to *The Morning Chat*. I'm Mike Redman. In today's programme, I want to know who does what jobs around your house! Our first caller is Erica. Hi Erica.

E: Hello Mike.

M: Erica, can you tell us who does the jobs around your house?

E: Well, my husband always cooks. He's a great cook! And he usually washes the dishes and cleans the kitchen. I usually clean the bathroom and I do the washing. Our two children feed and walk the dog. And we all go to the supermarket at the weekend.

M: Thanks Erica. That's great! Our next caller is Will. Hi Will.

W: Hi Mike!

M: Will, what jobs do you do around the house?

W: I always make breakfast and lunch, but my wife cooks dinner because I work in the evening. I'm a taxi driver. We usually clean the house at the weekend. I clean the bathroom and kitchen. Julia cleans the bedrooms, makes the beds and cleans the windows.

M: Thanks Will. Our last caller is Kelly. Kelly, who cooks dinner in your house?

K: Hi Mike. I always cook dinner. And I make breakfast and lunch. I live with my sister and she never cooks.

M: Ha ha! Who cleans the bathroom?

K: I clean the bathroom, and the kitchen, and the floors! And I do the washing. My sister is very busy. She's got two jobs. She doesn't work at weekends and then she makes great cakes!

M: Thanks Kelly. That sounds great!

UNIT 7 Recording 1

P = Presenter   L = Lisa   B = Ben   J = John   S = Sara

P: Welcome to the *Travel Tales* podcast. Today's podcast is about good and bad holidays. Lisa, how was your last holiday?

L: My last holiday was in May. I was in Thailand with my parents and my daughter. We were on an island in the south of Thailand and our hotel was next to the sea. There were lots of restaurants and the food was great! We were very happy.

P: How about you, Ben? Was your last holiday good?

B: My last holiday wasn't very good. It was in February. I was with my wife in a small town in Hungary. The train was busy and slow. The hotel was old and cold at night. There wasn't a restaurant in the hotel and there was only one restaurant in the town. The food wasn't very good. It was my wife's 40th birthday and she wasn't happy!

P: Oh no! That isn't good! John, how was your last holiday?

J: My last holiday was great! I was in Paris for the weekend with my sister in July. The train was really fast and cheap. Our hotel was near the museums and lots of really good restaurants. The food was very good! It was a short holiday, but it was really great.

P: Great! Finally, Sara, how was your last holiday?

S: My last holiday was really bad. I was in London for a week last November. It was very cold and dark. The hotel was very old and it wasn't clean. The restaurants were expensive and the food wasn't good. The buses and trains were expensive and taxis were difficult to find.

UNIT 8   Recording 1

Z = Zoe   P = Paul

Z: I don't know what to do at the weekend. It's my sister's birthday and I want to do something special. Have you got any ideas?

P: What does she like doing? Watching films? Music?

Z: Erm, she likes music and dancing. She doesn't really like the cinema.

P: Hmmm, what about the dance festival? It's on this weekend.

Z: The dance festival?

P: Yes, it's in Meadow Park every year in June. My friend Katy and I went last year – it was great!

Z: Oh yeah? What did you do there?

P: We watched lots of dancing from different countries and we ate some amazing food.

Z: Oh, that sounds fun! Was it a big event?

P: Yes, it was. There were dancers from about 20 countries. They all wore amazing, traditional clothes – lots of different colours.

Z: Wow!

P: And we listened to lots of great music. I really liked the Mexican music.

Z: Did you learn any dances?

P: Yes, I learnt some Turkish dances and samba from Brazil.

Z: Were there lots of people there?

P: Yes, there were. It was very busy.

Z: Was it expensive?

P: Well, the festival was free, but the food and drink were quite expensive.

Z: What did you eat?

P: I had *Feijoada* – it's from Brazil – and Katy had some Thai food.

Z: Were you at the festival all day?

P: Yes. It started at 10 o'clock in the morning and finished at 11 o'clock at night!

Z: Wow, that's late!

P: Yeah, I was really tired the next day, but I had a great time!

Z: OK. The dance festival's a great idea for my sister's birthday. Where do I get the tickets?

P: You can get them online.

Z: Cool. Thanks, Paul!

UNIT 9   Recording 1

P = Presenter   S = Sofia   M = Marta   O = Onur   G = Guy

P: Welcome to *Study Skills*! In today's podcast, we ask, 'Do you like learning English?' Sofia.

S: I love learning new languages and I love taking exams – I always pass them! I usually sit at the front of my English class and I write everything the teacher says in my notebook. I like reading books and newspapers in English and I love watching TV programmes in English, too. I don't like looking at my phone screen for a long time, so I don't use any apps for learning English.

P: Marta.

M: I like learning English, but it isn't easy! I always do my homework, but I can never remember words in English.

I never use a notebook because I use my phone to write notes. I use a dictionary app on my phone, too. I enjoy watching TV programmes and films in English, but I don't always understand them. I don't like reading books in English.

P: Onur.

O: I don't usually like studying or learning English and I never read books in English or do my homework. But last year, I took a two-week course in Brighton in the south of England and I loved it! Our teacher was great. We played lots of games and spoke English all the time. We learnt lots of new things, but it was fun and it wasn't boring! At the end of the course, we took an exam and I knew all of the answers! I usually hate taking exams and I always fail them, but I passed 100 percent!

P: Guy.

G: I love travelling and I like learning English because I can speak to people from lots of different countries, but I don't really like studying. I don't like doing homework and I hate going to the library. It's always quiet in the library and I can't talk to my friends. I like using the internet to talk to people or watch films.

UNIT 10   Recording 1

S = Sabrina   J = Jack

S: What are you going to do next year, Jack? Are you going to go to university?

J: No, I'm not. I'm going to travel around India.

S: Wow! That sounds great! I'd love to go to India. How long are you going to go for?

J: I don't know. I'm going to leave in July when we finish school, but I don't know when I'm going to come home again.

S: Who are you going to go with?

J: Two friends from my football club.

S: And which places are you going to visit in India?

J: Well, I'd like to see the mountains in the north. And I'd like to visit the Taj Mahal.

S: Oh yes, I'd love to see the Taj Mahal! You're going to have a great time! What are you going to do after your trip to India?

J: I'm going to study painting at art college. I love painting and taking photos. I'd like to be an art teacher. What about you? What are you going to do after school?

S: I'd like to join the police, but I'm going to go to university first.

J: Yeah? What are you going to study?

S: English.

J: Which university are you going to study at?

S: I'm going to go to Birmingham.

J: Really? I'm going to study there, too! When does your course start?

S: In the autumn. I'm going to work here in the summer first, in a supermarket.

J: Oh? Are you going to work all summer?

S: No, I'm not. I'd like to go on holiday!

J: Where would you like to go?

S: Italy – I love Italian food!

UNIT 1

1A

1
1 Canada 2 Mexico 3 Thailand 4 Poland 5 Argentina
6 Spain

2
1 the UK 2 Türkiye 3 Mexico 4 Argentina 5 Spain
6 the US 7 Canada 8 Japan

3
1 Spain 2 Argentina 3 Mexico 4 Poland 5 Canada
6 Japan

4
1 Are you John?
2 I'm from Türkiye.
3 You aren't late.
4 Where are you from?
5 I'm not a teacher.
6 Am I on time?
7 Are you from Canada?
8 I'm not from the UK.

5
1 A: Where ~~is~~ **are** you from Inés?
  B: I'm from Mexico.
2 A: Are you a student?
  B: No, ~~I~~ **I'm** not.
3 A: Am I late?
  B: No, ~~you~~ **you're** not.
4 A: Are you Mehmet?
  B: Yes, I ~~are~~ **am**.
5 A: ~~Am~~ **Are** you from Türkiye?
  B: No, I'm not.
6 A: Are you from the US?
  B: Yes, ~~I'm~~ **I am**.
7 A: Where are you from?
  B: ~~I~~ **I'm** from Spain.
8 A: ~~You are~~ **Are you** a teacher?
  B: No, I'm a student.

6
1 I am
2 I'm not
3 you're not
4 I am
5 you're not
6 I am

1B

1
1 doctor 2 taxi driver 3 pilot 4 school teacher 5 nurse
6 football player 7 office worker 8 farmer

2

C	O	R	S	R	F	A	S	S	C	D	U	P	W
B	O	F	A	N	G	D	O	C	T	O	R	C	L
O	S	J	V	D	A	O	L	H	I	F	A	R	M
L	N	H	X	J	N	U	S	O	F	F	I	D	E
Q	U	P	K	D	E	M	G	O	O	I	L	S	T
Z	R	P	B	O	X	E	Y	L	T	C	E	L	A
H	S	B	L	F	K	E	R	T	B	E	L	Y	X
N	E	M	O	O	W	D	E	E	L	W	Y	R	I
G	L	P	I	L	O	T	L	A	P	O	S	F	D
S	C	K	E	R	R	D	A	C	O	R	N	N	R
S	D	F	A	R	M	E	R	H	I	K	D	X	I
M	A	N	G	C	R	T	A	E	O	E	L	L	V
I	B	S	L	K	Z	T	A	R	P	R	W	B	E
F	O	O	T	B	A	L	L	P	L	A	Y	E	R

3
1 office worker 2 doctor 3 school teacher 4 pilot
5 farmer 6 taxi driver

4
1 David isn't from Mexico. ~~It's~~ **He's** from Spain.
2 Sarah ~~are~~ **is** a teacher.
3 ~~He is~~ **Is he** a doctor?
4 A: Is Pablo a pilot?
  B: No, he ~~aren't~~ **isn't**.
5 ~~Where Isabel is~~ **Where is Isabel** from?
6 She ~~aren't~~ **isn't** a farmer.
7 A: Is Peter from the US?
  B: Yes, he ~~are~~ **is**.
8 It ~~are~~ **is** a small hospital.

5
1 Kate's from the UK.
2 John isn't a doctor. / John's not a doctor.
3 It isn't a small office. / It's not a small office.
4 Where's James from?
5 It's a small school.
6 He's a taxi driver.

6
1 He isn't a teacher.
2 Is she from Italy?
3 Is it a small hospital?
4 She's from Poland.
5 It isn't a small school. / It's not a small school.
6 She isn't a pilot. / She's not a pilot.
7 He's a nurse.
8 Where's she from?

1c

1

Countries	Nationalities
Canada	Canadian
Spain	Spanish
Türkiye	Turkish
Mexico	Mexican
the US	American
Poland	Polish
Japan	Japanese
the UK	British
Argentina	Argentinian
Thailand	Thai
Brazil	Brazilian
Italy	Italian

2
1 the US 2 Polish 3 Mexican 4 Brazil 5 Canada 6 Italian
7 Argentina 8 the UK 9 Türkiye 10 Spain 11 Thailand
12 Japanese

3
1 Japan 2 Argentinian 3 Spanish 4 Canada 5 British
6 Mexican

4
1 aren't 2 are 3 are 4 are 5 aren't 6 are 7 Are
8 Are

5
1 aren't British. 2 are they from 3 Are you friends?
4 are the boys 5 aren't Turkish 6 aren't nurses

6
1 **A:** Are Maria and Anna sisters? **B:** No, they're housemates.
2 **A:** Are you and Simon Spanish **B:** No, we're from Argentina.
3 **A:** Who are they? **B:** They're my friends.
4 **A:** Are we late? **B:** No, you're on time.

1d

1
1 d 2 e 3 a 4 f 5 b 6 c

2
1 ~~What~~ **What's** your first name?
2 What's ~~you~~ **your** family name?
3 ~~How's~~ **What's** your phone number?
4 What's your email ~~number~~ **address**?
5 How **do** you spell that?
6 ~~Me~~ **My** family name is Demir.
7 My phone number ~~are~~ **is** 07820 511 370.
8 Sorry, can ~~your~~ **you** say that again?

3
1 What's your name?
2 How do you spell your first name?
3 How do you spell your family name?
4 What's your phone number?
5 Sorry, can you say that again?
6 What's your email address?

Listening

1
1 a language school
2 a hospital
3 an international conference

2
student nurse doctor manager teacher office worker

3a

Name	Nationality	Job
Lucia	Argentinian	student
Gosia	Polish	office worker
Maria	Brazilian	student nurse
David	Brazilian	student nurse
Sarah	British	student doctor
Pete	British	teacher
Cristina	Spanish	manager

4a
1 F 2 F 3 T 4 T 5 T 6 T 7 F 8 F

Reading

1
1 b 2 c

2
1 Mi Na 2 Gabriela 3 Gabriela 4 Steve 5 Matteo
6 Lesley 7 Jenny 8 Lesley 9 Matteo 10 Mi Na

3
1 F 2 F 3 T 4 F 5 F 6 F 7 T 8 T

4
1 student, manager, teacher, office worker, nurse, pilot.
2 the UK, Canada, Brazil, South Korea, Italy
3 American, English

Writing

1

Name	City	Country	Nationality	Job
Sara Demir	Istanbul	Türkiye	Turkish	doctor
Matthew Turner	Manchester	the UK	British	office worker
Sandra Fernandez	Buenos Aires	Argentina	Argentinian	English teacher
David Nowak	Warsaw	Poland	Polish	taxi driver

3
1 Becky isn't from the US. She's from Canada.
2 My name is Peter. I'm from London.
3 Jane and I aren't sisters. We're housemates.
4 My mother is Polish and my father is from Italy.
5 Antoni is a football player.
6 Jose and Pablo are in the same class.

4
1 Hello / Hi. I'm Gloria Lopez / My name is Gloria Lopez.
   I'm from Mexico City in Mexico. I'm a doctor.
2 Hello / Hi. I'm Charlie Suparat / My name is Charlie Suparat.
   I'm from Bangkok in Thailand. I'm a student.

5–6
Students' own answers.

2A

1
1 mother   2 mum   3 son   4 father   5 husband   6 dad
7 sister   8 brother   9 daughter   10 wife

2
♂ 1–5   father, dad, husband, son, brother
♀ 6–10   mother, mum, wife, daughter, sister

3
1 husband   2 brother   3 sister   4 father   5 mother/mum
6 wife   7 daughter   8 son

4
1 Their   2 Jacob's   3 Our   4 George's   5 Its   6 His
7 son's   8 Her

5
1 My mother's mother is from Argentina.
2 Lucy is Daniel's sister.
3 My cat's name is Pixie.
4 Oliver's wife is a nurse.
5 His daughter's name is Elizabeth.
6 Sandra is Jon's wife.
7 My husband's mother and father are farmers.
8 What's your friend's name?

6
1 her   2 Our   3 His   4 Their   5 Its   6 your   7 My   8 Her

2B

1
1 table   2 chair   3 phone   4 pen   5 clock   6 cup   7 desk
8 computer   9 key   10 photo   11 book   12 box

2
phone, pen, cup, desk, computer

3
1 clock   2 desk   3 chair   4 key   5 book   6 box

4
1 These are desks.
2 These are chairs.
3 These are photos.
4 These are watches.
5 These are keys.
6 These are boxes.
7 These are phones.
8 These are families.

5

	Near (here)	Far (there)
Singular	this	that
Plural	these	those

6
1 These   2 these   3 that   4 That   5 this   6 This   7 this
8 Those   9 that   10 that

7
1 This   2 these   3 that   4 those

2C

1
12   twelve
14   fourteen
16   sixteen
11   eleven
19   nineteen
18   eighteen
13   thirteen
20   twenty
15   fifteen
17   seventeen

2
1 fifty   2 twelve   3 thirteen   4 a hundred/one hundred
5 fifteen   6 ninety   7 thirty   8 eleven   9 seventeen
10 nineteen   11 twenty   12 seventy

3
Students' own answers.

4
1 What   2 How   3 Where   4 What   5 How   6 What
7 Who   8 Where

5
1 Where are they from?
2 What's his job?
3 Where are you from?
4 How old are they?
5 What's your name?
6 How old is your sister?
7 What's your phone number?
8 Who are those people over there?

6
1 What's   2 Where   3 How   4 Who's   5 What's   6 What's

2D

1
1 d   2 i   3 e   4 h   5 a   6 c   7 g   8 b   9 f   10 j

2

Customer's phrases	Shop assistant's phrases
How much is that?	It's £12.
How much is this book?	Cash or card?
Here you are.	Here's your change.
Can I pay by card?	That's £27.99, please.
How much are those cups?	
Here's my card.	

3
1
1 help   2 much   3 those   4 that   5 card   6 Here
7 change   8 Excuse   9 It's   10 how   11 That's   12 pay
13 you   14 card

Listening

1
1 a   2 a   3 b

2
1 phone, 8 camera, 5 computer, 9 photos, 3 credit card, 6 cash,
4 book, 7 passport, 2 keys

3
1 c   2 a   3 b

Reading

1
Kelly C   Sara A   Yui B

2
1 T   2 F   3 F   4 T   5 F   6 F   7 T   8 F

3
1 parents'   2 sister   3 mother   4 son   5 father   6 husband
7 children   8 daughter

4
5, 6, 8, 18, 21, 22, 24, 26, 30, 37, 65, 67, 70

Writing

1
1 first name   2 Lodz   3 date of birth   4 pilot   5 River Street
6 post code

2
twenty-second of July 1989

3
1 first name   2 surname   3 address   4 phone number
5 email address   6 DOB   7 occupation   8 signature

4
1 Rob
2 Schmidt
3 330 Queen Street, Cambridge, CB12 2ED
4 07343 211 498
5 schmidt.rr@abcmail.com
6 12/08/1988
7 taxi driver

5
Students' own answers.

UNIT 3

1
Across
2 flat   5 house   7 cinema   8 park   10 hotel
11 supermarket   12 restaurant
Down
1 café   3 train station   4 bookshop   6 market   8 bank

2
1 bookshop   2 train station   3 park   4 restaurant
5 supermarket   6 cinema

3
1 There are   2 There aren't   3 There are   4 There isn't
5 There is   6 There are   7 There isn't   8 There are
9 There aren't   10 There is

4
1 There is a cinema.
2 There are two bookshops.
3 There aren't any parks.
4 There isn't a bank in my town.
5 The aren't any hotels in my town.
6 There are no supermarkets here.
7 There aren't any train stations in my town.
8 There are four cafés in my town.

5
1 there are   2 There are   3 There is/There isn't
4 There aren't   5 There is   6 There are   7 There are
8 There are

1

Rooms in a house	Things in a house
living room bathroom bedroom kitchen	toilet oven shower sofa lift table bed TV

2
1 living room   2 kitchen   3 bathroom   4 bedroom

3
1 sofa, TV, table   2 oven, table, chairs   3 shower, toilet
4 bed

4
1 toilet   2 kitchen   3 beds   4 living   5 lift   6 table

5
1 Is there   2 are there   3 rooms   4 Are there   5 Is there
6 Is there   7 Are there   8 floors

6
1 a   2 d   3 b   4 c   5 e   6 g   7 f   8 h

7
1 There are   2 There's   3 Is there   4 there is   5 is there
6 there isn't   7 Is there   8 there isn't   9 Are there
10 there are

1
1 big   2 quiet   3 small   4 expensive   5 cheap   6 bad
7 busy   8 new   9 good   10 old

2

old	new
quiet	busy
good	bad
expensive	cheap
big	small

3
1 small   2 old   3 quiet   4 expensive   5 bad   6 big
7 new   8 busy   9 cheap   10 good

4
1 Is there a big park?
2 That is a good bookshop.
3 There are two new supermarkets.
4 My flat is small.
5 There's a busy market.
6 It is a bad restaurant.
7 This is a quiet town.
8 There aren't any expensive restaurants.
9 Is there a cheap hotel in this town.
10 Are there any old houses in this town?

5
1 That cinema is old.
2 The train station is busy.
3 Is that restaurant expensive?
4 Is the bank small?
5 The bookshop is not new.
6 Are there any cheap supermarkets?
7 Is your town's market big?
8 Is the park in your town big?
9 Simon's flat is not big.
10 Are there any good hotels in your town?

3D

1
1 near 2 one 3 down 4 past 5 at 6 on 7 Where's
8 on 9 straight 10 after 11 down

2
1 Is there a supermarket near here?
2 Go past the cinema.
3 Go down South Street.
4 There's a bank on Station Road.
5 Turn left at the park.
6 Go past the school.
7 The restaurant is on the right.
8 It's next to a park.

Listening

1
one

2
hospital park bookshop supermarket train station
Spanish restaurant university hotel café offices

3
1 Mexican 2 big 3 expensive 4 school 5 restaurants
6 market 7 isn't 8 There isn't 9 are 10 university
11 small 12 busy

4
Speaker 1
great big good new expensive
Speaker 2
small cheap old quiet
Speaker 3
big good great small busy

Reading

1
c

2
1 Metro Hotel 2 City Flat 3 Grand Hotel

3
1 F 2 T 3 F 4 F 5 F 6 F 7 T 8 F 9 T 10 T

4
1 isn't 2 isn't 3 aren't any 4 isn't 5 is 6 isn't 7 is
8 are

5

Rooms in the house
bedroom bathroom kitchen living room
Things in the house
bed shower oven wifi
Places in town
café restaurant train station market park bookshop

Writing

1
1 a 2 b 3 b 4 b 5 a 6 b 7 b 8 a

3
1 There is a big kitchen **and** there is a big living room.
2 There isn't a bath in the bathroom, **but** there's a shower.
3 There's a market, but there **isn't** a supermarket.
4 The market is very good **and** it's cheap.
5 There isn't a TV, **but** there's a radio.
6 There are two bedrooms, but there **isn't** a living room.

4
1 d 2 f 3 a 4 b 5 c 6 e

5–6
Students' own answers.

UNIT 4

4A

1
1 in her 20s 2 brown 3 blue 4 grey 5 in his 30s 6 beard

2
Down
1 beard 2 hair 3 blonde
Across
3 blue 4 brown 5 eyes

3
1 have got 2 hasn't got 3 has got 4 haven't got 5 has got
6 have got 7 has got 8 have got

4
1 Sophie hasn't got a phone.
2 I haven't got a pen.
3 We've got a big house.
4 They haven't got any books.
5 David's got four dogs.
6 My desk hasn't got a chair.
7 Sonia's got a black car.
8 Isobel hasn't got a watch.

5
1 I've got blue eyes. I haven't got brown hair.
2 Rob's got blonde hair. He hasn't got green hair.
3 Eva's got a bed. She hasn't got a sofa.
4 Matt's town has got a cinema. It hasn't got a market.
5 My husband and I have got a small house. We haven't got a clock.
6 Andy and Tim have got a big flat. They haven't got a table.

4B

1
1 passport 2 bag 3 bottle of water 4 food 5 credit card
6 tickets 7 house keys 8 camera 9 sunglasses 10 phone
11 coat 12 money

2
1 a newspaper 2 money 3 a ticket 4 a coat 5 a camera
6 a bottle of water

3
1 Have; got; haven't
2 Have; got; have
3 Have; got; have
4 Has; got; hasn't
5 Have; got; have
6 Has; got; has

4

1 ~~Has~~ **Have** you got your passport?
2 ~~You have~~ **Have you** got a ticket?
3 Has she **got** a new camera?
4 Yes, ~~he's got~~ **he has**.
5 ~~Is~~ **Has** Susan got food?
6 ~~Has~~ **Have** they got their coats?
7 No, I **haven't** ~~got~~.
8 Have you ~~get~~ **got** a new phone?

5

1 Has George got a new coat?
   No, he hasn't.
2 Has your flat got a lift?
   Yes, it has.
3 Have you got brothers or sisters?
   No, I haven't.
4 Have you got the tickets?
   Yes, I have.
5 Have they got a big house?
   No, they haven't.
6 Has he got an expensive camera?
   Yes, he has.

4C

1

1 take 2 drink 3 visit 4 go 5 see 6 try 7 take 8 buy

2

1 b 2 b 3 b 4 a 5 b 6 a 7 a 8 b

3

1 b 2 e 3 h 4 a 5 c 6 g 7 d 8 f

4

1 Don't ~~visits~~ Buckingham Palace!
2 ~~Drinks~~ lots of water.
3 ~~Doesn't~~ **Don't** buy coffee there. It's expensive!
4 Don't ~~goes~~ **go** to that supermarket. It's very busy.
5 ~~Not~~ **Don't** visit the town. It's not good for holidays.
6 ~~Sees~~ that show. It's very good!
7 ~~Not~~ **Don't** try the tea in that restaurant.
8 ~~Takes~~ lots of photos!

5

1 Don't buy 2 Don't drink 3 See 4 Try 5 Don't talk
6 Take

4D

1

1 09.35 2 18.45 3 05.30 4 12.20 5 14.10 6 16.15
7 07.40 8 11.00 9 01.05 10 03.50

2

1 eleven o'clock 2 twenty past twelve 3 twenty to eight
4 five past one 5 quarter to seven 5 quarter past four

3

1 it 2 o'clock 3 late 4 time 5 at 6 Seven 7 six 8 is
9 past 10 thirty

Listening

1

a a hotel b airport

2

at the (Plaza) hotel

3

1 beard 2 blue 3 50 4 brown 5 black

4

A

Reading

1

Tokyo

2

A 6 B 1 C 4 D 2 E 3 F 5

3

1 Yoshi 2 Yoshi 3 taxis 4 Asakusa, Harajuku park
5 (type of) Japanese food 6 January

Writing

1

1 F 2 T 3 T 4 F 5 F 6 F

3

1 I've got a book, a map, a camera and a passport.
2 Have you got the tickets?
3 Kirsty's coat is black.
4 Laura hasn't got a computer.
5 I've got a letter, but I haven't got a stamp.
6 We've got some food and water.

4

Hi Alicia,

How are you? I'm great. I've got some American money and my mum's credit card. I haven't got a camera, but my phone's got a good camera. I've got a map of New York City, a map of the subway and a map of the airport. I've got a bag for the plane with some food, water, a book and a newspaper.

See you next week,
Magda

5–6

Students' own answers.

UNIT 5

5A

1

1 Sunday 2 Monday 3 Friday 4 Tuesday 5 Thursday
6 Saturday 7 Wednesday

2

1 Monday 2 Saturday 3 Tuesday 4 Friday 5 Wednesday
6 Sunday 7 Thursday

3

1 go 2 have 3 have 4 go 5 go 6 have

4

1 get up 2 watch 3 work 4 have 5 go 6 go to
7 study 8 go

5

1 I 2 don't 3 don't 4 have dinner 5 They 6 don't

6

1 on 2 from 3 At 4 to 5 on 6 at

7

1 I have dinner with my family on Sundays /
On Sundays, I have dinner with my family.
2 I don't have lunch on Tuesdays /
On Tuesdays, I don't have lunch.
3 I don't work on Fridays or Saturdays.
4 On Saturdays, we study from 7.30 to 9.30 /
We study from 7.30 to 9.30 on Saturdays.
5 We go to the cinema on Saturdays /
On Saturdays, we go to the cinema.
6 I work in a supermarket from Monday to Friday /
From Monday to Friday, I work in a supermarket.

1

1 boat 2 train 3 plane 4 taxi 5 car 6 bus 7 bike

2

1 e 2 c 3 f 4 b 5 a 6 d 7 h 8 g

3

1 leave 2 walk 3 travel 4 take 5 arrive 6 arrive
7 leave 8 ride

4

1 Do you take the bus to work?
2 What time do you leave home?
3 How do you travel to your office?
4 What time do your brothers arrive home?
5 Do you ride your bike to school?
6 Do your friends drive to university?
7 How do your children travel to school?
8 Do you and your family walk to the supermarket?

5

1 c 2 g 3 e 4 h 5 b 6 d 7 f 8 a

6

1 Do; don't 2 Do; do 3 What; do 4 Do; don't 5 How do
6 Do; don't

1

Across

2 meat 5 chicken 7 bread 8 sandwich 9 cake 10 sugar
11 coffee 13 salad

Down

1 fish 2 milk 3 tea 4 cheese 6 chocolate 12 eggs

2

Food	Drinks
chicken cheese cake bread sugar eggs salad meat fish sandwich chocolate	milk coffee tea

3

1 coffee 2 sugar 3 meat 4 milk 5 salad 6 eat

4

1 I am never late for work.
2 We sometimes have meat for dinner.
3 My children often eat chocolate after lunch.
4 I always have a cup of coffee with breakfast.
5 I usually cycle to work.
6 We often eat healthy food.
7 I sometimes have tea and cake in a restaurant.
8 We are usually at home for lunch on Sundays.

5

1 I ~~sometimes am~~ **am sometimes** late for work.
2 How often **do** you eat chocolate?
3 We ~~eat usually~~ **usually eat** lunch in a restaurant.
4 ~~Always I~~ **I always** have dinner with my family.
5 I **never** go to bed late ~~never~~.
6 We **are** always ~~are~~ at home for dinner.
7 My friends ~~buy usually~~ **usually buy** sandwiches for lunch.
8 I ~~eat often~~ **often eat** lunch at my desk.

1

1 g 2 e 3 h 4 d 5 f 6 b 7 c 8 j 9 a 10 i

2

1 what 2 egg 3 Would 4 drink 5 cup 6 milk 7 like
8 much 9 That's 10 welcome

Listening

1

three

2

car 2 boat 1 plane 3 bike 1 bus 4 taxi 2 train 3

3

	bike	car	taxi	bus	plane	boat	train	walk
1					✓		✓	
2	✓							✓
3			✓	✓				
4						✓	✓	
5				✓				
6			✓	✓			✓	

4

Speaker 1 sometimes
Speaker 2 never
Speaker 3 usually
Speaker 4 often
Speaker 5 always
Speaker 6 always

Reading

1

football player

2

1 f 2 g 3 e 4 a 5 c 6 b 7 d

3

1 F 2 T 3 F 4 T 5 F 6 F 7 F 8 T

4

1 eggs, cheese, bread, milk, coffee, tea
2 salad, cheese sandwich, green tea, cake, chocolate
3 chicken, fish

Writing

1
1 F   2 F   3 T   4 T   5 F   6 F

2
I'm a doctor at a hospital. I <u>usually</u> work from Monday to Friday, but I <u>sometimes</u> work on Saturdays and Sundays, too. I <u>always</u> get up at 7 o'clock. I have breakfast with my family and then I go to work at 8 o'clock. I usually cycle to work, but sometimes I take the bus. I <u>never</u> drive to work. I arrive at the hospital at 8.30. At 1 o'clock I have lunch. I <u>often</u> go to a café and I always have a cheese sandwich, a salad and a <u>big</u> cup of tea. The food is <u>good</u>, but the café is usually <u>busy</u>. I usually go home at 6.30, but sometimes I go to the gym first. At 8 o'clock I have dinner with my family. Then we often watch TV. I usually go to bed at 10 o'clock.

3
1 I am never late for work.
2 I usually get up at 9 o'clock on Sundays.
3 I always work from Monday to Friday.
4 Has the café got cheap food and drink?
5 I sometimes take the train to work.
6 I work in a small school.

4
1 I usually have breakfast at 8 o'clock.
2 Do you always work from Monday to Friday?
3 I usually take the train to work.
4 I sometimes go to a café for lunch.
5 I never watch TV after dinner.
6 Do you always cycle to school?

5–6
Students' own answers.

UNIT 6

6A

1
1 every day   2 in the morning   3 every week
4 in the afternoon   5 at the weekend   6 at night

2
1 in the evening   2 in the morning   3 at the weekend
4 at night   5 every day   6 in the afternoon   7 every week
8 at the weekend

3
1 Alicia **lives** in a small flat
2 Max **doesn't work** in a big office.
3 Fred **studies** English at the weekend.
4 Olivia **watches** TV in the evening.
5 Emily **doesn't have** eggs for breakfast.
6 Rafael **doesn't go** to work at 8 o'clock.
7 Sophie **finishes** work at 6 o'clock.
8 Henry **doesn't eat** lots of chocolate.

4
1 My sister **lives** in a small town in Mexico.
2 Dan **doesn't work** at the weekend.
3 Beth **doesn't wear** glasses.
4 My housemate **studies** English in the evening.
5 My parents **go** to bed at 10 o'clock every day.
6 Paolo starts work at 9 and **finishes** at 5.
7 I **have** a salad for lunch every day.
8 Sandy **goes** to work at 6 o'clock in the morning.

5
1 lives   2 works   3 gets up   4 leaves   5 doesn't have
6 takes   7 arrives   8 starts   9 has   10 finishes
11 goes   12 has   13 doesn't watch   14 studies   15 reads

6B

1
1 the washing   2 the dishes   3 breakfast   4 the washing
5 the kitchen   6 the beds   7 the children   8 the bathroom

2
1 cook   2 goes   3 clean up   4 feeds   5 clean   6 washes
7 do   8 makes

3
1 go   2 makes   3 do   4 cooks/makes   5 cleans
6 walk/feed   7 washes   8 washes/does

4
1 A: Does Ewa make her bed every day?
  B: No, she doesn't.
2 A: Where does Rebecca live?
3 A: Does he walk the dog?
  B: No, he doesn't.
4 A: Who does the washing in your house?
5 A: What does Leo do around the house?
6 A: How often does Julia clean the kitchen?
7 A: Does she clean the bathroom?
  B: Yes, she does.
8 A: Does he cook dinner?
  B: Yes, he does.

5
1 How often does Beth do the washing?
2 What jobs does Andy do around the house?
3 Does Mark walk the dog?
4 Who washes the dishes in your house?
5 When does the dog have dinner?
6 Where does Peter live?
7 Does Fatima work in an office?
8 How often does James cook dinner?

6
1 Where does Laura live?
2 How often does she clean the bathroom?
3 When does the train leave?
4 Does David cook dinner?
5 What (jobs) does Stef do around the house?
6 Does Alex walk the dog?

6C

1
1 build a website   2 swim   3 ride a horse   4 make a cake
5 dance   6 play football   7 make clothes   8 fly a plane
9 speak two languages   10 sleep on a train   11 sing
12 draw pictures

2
1 c   2 e   3 a   4 h   5 b   6 d   7 g   8 f

3
1 make   2 swims   3 flies   4 speaks   5 play   6 sleep
7 dance   8 makes

4
1 Daniel can ride a bike, but he can't ride a horse.
2 Leo can sing and dance very well.
3 I can play the piano, but I can't sing.
4 What can you cook?
5 Chloe can make cakes, but she can't cook very well.
6 How many languages can Flora speak?

5
1 Can; ride; can   2 can; speak; can speak   3 Can; drive; can't
4 Can; make; can; make   5 Can; cook; can't; can make
6 use; can build

6

1 Paul can speak German. Katy can speak Spanish.
2 Paul can't ride a horse. Katy can ride a horse.
3 Paul can fly a plane. Katy can't fly a plane.
4 Paul can cook. Katy can cook.
5 Paul can't play football. Katy can play football.
6 Paul can dance. Katy can dance.

1

1 Can I use your computer, please?
2 Yes, you can.
3 I'm sorry, you can't.
4 Can you wash the dishes, please?
5 Yes, I can.
6 No problem.

2

Making requests	Saying yes to requests	Saying no to requests
Can I use your computer, please?	Sure.	I'm sorry, I can't.
Can you wash the dishes, please?	Yes, I can.	I'm sorry, you can't.
	No problem.	

3

1 Can you do; Sure 2 Can I use; you can 3 Can you walk; I can't
4 Can you play; I'm sorry 5 Can I help; Yes
6 Can you wash; No problem

Listening

1
1 four 2 two 3 two

2
1 Erica's husband 2 Erica 3 Erica's children 4 Will's wife
5 Will 6 Will's wife 7 Kelly 8 Kelly

3
1 cleans the bathroom; does the washing; goes to the supermarket
2 cooks; washes the dishes; cleans the kitchen; goes to the supermarket
3 feed the dog; walk the dog; go to the supermarket
4 makes the breakfast and lunch; cleans the bathroom and kitchen
5 cooks dinner; cleans the bedrooms; makes the beds; cleans the windows
6 makes breakfast, lunch and dinner; cleans the bathroom, kitchen and floors; does the washing
7 makes cakes

Reading

1
Melissa lives with Lara.

2
1 F (Melissa is a great friend, but she isn't a great housemate.)
2 T
3 F (Melissa works at home.)
4 F (Melissa calls friends every night.)
5 F (Melissa can cook and make cakes.)
6 T
7 F (Melissa and Lara have got a dog.)
8 T

3
1 Lara 2 Melissa 3 Melissa 4 Lara 5 Melissa 6 Melissa

4
1 clean 2 call 3 go 4 wash 5 feed 6 do 7 make
8 work

Writing

1
1 in a school
2 at 5 o'clock in the evening
3 at 6 o'clock in the evening
4 Abby
5 at half past 10 at night
6 she cleans the bathroom
7 on Saturday afternoons
8 on Sunday mornings

2
1 At 5 o'clock in the evening, we finish work and go home.
2 At the weekend, we all do jobs around the house.
3 On Sunday mornings, we do the washing.
4 Eduardo makes dinner at 6 o'clock.
5 I take the dog for a walk in the afternoon.
6 We all work in a school from Monday to Friday.

3
1 on 2 at 3 on 4 at 5 in 6 at 7 in 8 at

4
1 From Monday **to** Saturday, Joseph works in a hospital.
2 Alison feeds the dog **at** 7 o'clock in the morning.
3 We always go to the supermarket **at** the weekend.
4 Jenny does the washing **on** Saturday mornings.
5 I usually go to bed at 12 o'clock **at** night.
6 **At** 8 o'clock, Alex always has breakfast.

5–6
Students' own answers.

UNIT 7

1

Across
1 east 6 flowers 7 sea 8 north 10 hills 11 west
12 clouds
Down
2 trees 3 mountains 4 island 5 lake 6 fields 7 south
9 river

2
1 sky 2 sea 3 river 4 clouds 5 island 6 lake 7 sky
8 trees

3
1 trees 2 south 3 clouds 4 flowers 5 lake 6 river
7 mountains 8 island

4
1 How many 2 When 3 How 4 How much 5 When
6 What 7 Who 8 How many 8 Where

5
1 **Who** do you live with?
2 ✓
3 **How** many trees are in the park?
4 How **much** is it?
5 ✓
6 **How** do you spell the name of the hotel?
7 How **many** people do you live with?
8 **Where** are you from?

6

1 How much is the red car?
2 When does John start work?
3 How does Greg travel to school?
4 When is Amy's birthday?
5 What is your job?
6 Who does the washing in your house?

7

1 c 2 d 3 e 4 b 5 f 6 a

 7B

1

1 January 2 May 3 March 4 November 5 June 6 April
7 August 8 February

2

1 January 2 February 3 March 4 April 5 May 6 June
7 July 8 August 9 September 10 October 11 November
12 December

3

1 4th 2 12th 3 22nd 4 1st 5 13th 6 11th 7 30th
8 2nd 9 5th 10 13th

4

1 the second of November 2 the nineteenth of May
3 the twenty-second of July 4 the twenty-ninth of January
5 the first of March 6 the sixteenth of June
7 the twenty-fourth of April 8 the eleventh of December

5

1 It was Jack's birthday.
2 The restaurant was busy.
3 We were on holiday.
4 The hotel wasn't quiet.
5 There were ten people in my office.
6 There weren't any people on the boat.
7 They were at the cinema.
8 You weren't at work.

6

1 It **was** my birthday last week.
2 The restaurant **was** quiet yesterday.
3 There **were** lots of people at the party last night.
4 Ali and I **were** at the cinema last Saturday.
5 Esme **wasn't** at work yesterday.
6 The hotel **was** very expensive.
7 The food **was** great at Lorna's party.
8 My brothers **were** on holiday last month.

7

1 was 2 was 3 were 4 were 5 was 6 was 7 weren't
8 was 9 wasn't 10 wasn't 11 were 12 was 13 were
14 was

7C

1

1 hot 2 light 3 difficult 4 fast 5 sad 6 high 7 long
8 old

2

1 long 2 high 3 young 4 low 5 slow 6 difficult 7 cold
8 dark

3

1 hot 2 long 3 happy 4 high 5 young 6 fast 7 dark
8 difficult

4

1 A: Were you on holiday last week?
2 A: Was the hotel expensive?
3 B: It was £3.80.
4 A: Was Susan at home last night?
5 A: Where was Luke yesterday morning?
6 B: No, there wasn't.
7 A: Were Joanne and Katie at school yesterday?
8 A: How many people were at the meeting?

5

1 were; was 2 was; was 3 was; was 4 Was; wasn't; was
5 were; were 6 Were; weren't; were 7 was; was 8 Was; wasn't

7D

1

9 A: Thank you. What platform is the train to Dublin, please?
6 B: Is that a single or return?
11 A: Thank you.
4 B: It arrives at 12.30. The fast train leaves at 10 o'clock and arrives at 12.15.
7 A: A return, please.
8 B: That's £62.50, please.
3 A: What time does it arrive in Dublin?
10 B: It leaves from platform 11.
5 A: OK. A ticket for the fast train, please.
2 B: The next train leaves at 9.20. It's a slow train.
1 A: Excuse me. What time is the next train to Dublin?

2

1 tickets 2 return 3 That 4 time 5 is 6 arrive
7 platform 8 leaves

Listening

1

two

2

busy cheap cold dark expensive fast good great
happy old short slow

3

1 Sara 2 Lisa 3 John 4 Ben 5 Lisa 6 Ben 7 Ben
8 John

4a

1 F 2 T 3 F 4 F 5 T 6 F 7 F 8 T

Reading

1

in the east of an island in the Mediterranean Sea

2

1 50,000 2 July and August
3 swim in the sea and walk in the mountains 4 10,000
5 two every week 6 one

3

1 east 2 busy 3 taxis 4 are 5 weren't 6 trees
7 weren't 8 different countries

4

1 slow 2 hot 3 young 4 high 5 busy 6 big

Writing

1

a 2 b 6 c 1 d 4 e 5 f 3

2

1 First 2 Next/Then/After that 3 Next/Then/After that
4 Next/Then/After that 5 Finally

3
1 First 2 Next/Then/After that 3 Next/Then/After that
4 Next/Then/After that 5 Finally 6 First
7 Next/Then/After that 8 Next/Then/After that
9 Next/Then/After that 10 Finally

4

Type of transport	From	To
Train	Waterloo Station	Southampton Central
Walk	Southampton Central	Central Bus Station
Bus	Central Bus Station	boat terminal
Boat	boat terminal	West Cowes boat terminal
Walk	West Cowes boat terminal	Quayside bus stop
Bus	Quayside bus stop	Newport Bus Station
Taxi	Newport Bus Station	Blackwater Hotel

5
Students' own answers.

UNIT 8

8A

1
1 lived 2 travelled 3 played 4 loved 5 didn't like
6 watched 7 talked

2
1 d 2 e 3 a 4 b 5 f 6 c

3
1 lived 2 talked 3 travelled 4 watched 5 played 6 lived

4
1 visited 2 didn't like 3 cycled 4 didn't learn 5 lived
6 changed 7 didn't listen to 8 didn't watch

5
1 David **started** work early yesterday.
2 Ellie **studied** English at university.
3 I **didn't work** yesterday.
4 ✓
5 Classes **stopped** at 3 o'clock at my school.
6 The train **arrived** late yesterday.
7 ✓
8 I **didn't clean** my house yesterday.

6
1 I didn't travel to school by train.
2 Fiona didn't like the food in the restaurant.
3 Peter finished work at 6 o'clock.
4 I talked to my brother on Sunday.
5 Jess didn't clean the bathroom.
6 I studied in the afternoon.
7 They walked to school every day.
8 I tried new food on holiday.

8B

1
1 bought 2 got up 3 ran 4 met 5 felt 6 spoke
7 forgot 8 ate

2
1 met 2 didn't forget 3 didn't take 4 lost 5 had 6 went
7 didn't speak 8 broke

3
1 got up 2 had/ate 3 spoke 4 took 5 met 6 ran
7 went 8 ate/had 9 went 10 bought

4
Across
3 lost 5 bought 6 felt 7 took 10 spoke
Down
1 met 2 forgot 4 got up 5 broke

5
1 Yesterday, I **didn't get up** early.
2 Rob's phone **broke** yesterday.
3 Yuki **didn't eat** breakfast when she was young.
4 My sister **went** to the cinema last night.
5 I **didn't make** a cake for my dad's birthday – my sister did.
6 Greg **bought** a new computer last week.
7 Alison **lost** her money this morning.
8 I **didn't run** in the park last Saturday.

6
1 had 2 didn't go 3 didn't get up 4 went 5 made 6 was
7 ate 8 forgot 9 bought

8C

1
1 swim 2 went 3 stayed 4 go 5 went 6 have 7 visit
8 relaxed

2
1 went 2 visit 3 swam/went 4 go 5 stay
6 relaxed/stayed 7 had 8 went 9 visited 10 stayed

3
1 Yes 2 didn't 3 Yes 4 did 5 didn't 6 he did
7 they didn't 8 No

4
1 How 2 Where 3 When 4 How 5 What 6 What
7 Where 8 What

5
1 Where did you go on holiday last year? 2 When did you go?
3 Who did you go with? 4 How did you travel there?
5 What did you see? 6 What did you eat?

8D

1
1 Hi 2 How 3 good 4 great 5 OK
6 See 7 afternoon 8 well 9 thank you 10 Goodbye

2

Starting a conversation	Hello. Hi. Good morning. Good afternoon. Good evening.
Questions for greetings	How are you? How are things? Are you OK?
Answers for greetings	I'm fine, thanks. And you? I'm OK, thanks. And you? I'm not bad, thank you. And you? I'm great, thank you. And you? Very well, thank you. And you? I'm good, thank you. And you?
Ending a conversation	Goodbye. Bye. See you later. See you.

3
1 are 2 bad 3 was 4 How 5 went 6 Did 7 didn't
8 later

Listening

1
1 b

2a
1 b 2 a 3 a 4 a 5 b 6 a 7 a 8 b

3a
1 in Meadow Park 2 (about) 20 3 food from Brazil
4 11 o'clock at night 5 online

Reading

1
a good day

2
Regular verbs:
started walked listened
Irregular verbs:
got up was had ate drank took met ran
went for a walk bought spoke sat

3
A He didn't take the bus.
B He went to the park.
C He had a slow breakfast at the kitchen table.
D Peter didn't break anything.
E He didn't go to a busy restaurant.
F (Peter went home and) he sat in the garden.
G Peter didn't want to run.
H He didn't watch the TV.

Writing

1b
Malaga (Photo A)

2a
- What was the event?
  A holiday in Malaga.
- When was it?
  2017
- Where was it?
  Malaga, South of Spain
- Who was there?
  The writer's family – parents, brother and sister
- What happened?
  They had breakfast in a café; they went to the beach;
  they visited places in Malaga.
- Why was the event good/bad?
  It was good because they forgot problems and they relaxed.
  How did people feel after the event?
  The writer felt sad because the holiday was finished.

b
My favourite holiday was in Spain in 2017. We went to Malaga.
It's a small city in the south of Spain. We stayed there for two
weeks. I went with my family – my parents, my brother Toni and
my sister, Clara.
We stayed in a nice hotel near the sea. Every morning we went to a
café for breakfast – the coffee was so good! Then, we went to the
beach and relaxed.
On the last day, it rained so we went shopping. After breakfast,
we took a bus to the shops and bought lots of things. In the
afternoon, we visited the Picasso Museum. In the evening, we
were tired and went to bed early!
It was a great holiday. We forgot our problems. After the holiday,
I felt sad. I often think about Malaga.

3
1 a 2 f 3 d 4 b 5 g 6 e 7 c

4–5
Students' own answers.

 9A

1
1 c 2 b 3 b 4 a 5 c 6 a 7 c 8 b

2
1 There's a sofa **between** the bookcase and the table.
2 I worked **at** home on Thursday.
3 The train station is **in** front of the park.
4 We play football **in/at** the park every weekend.
5 I can't find my keys. I put them **on** the table, but they aren't there.
6 Can you clean up your bedroom please? Your clothes are **on**
the floor.

3
1 c 2 d 3 f 4 e 5 g 6 a 7 b

4
1 me 2 We 3 She 4 I 5 us 6 He 7 us 8 It 9 he
10 it

5
1 them 2 He 3 I 4 us 5 her 6 them 7 it 8 it/her/him

 9B

1
1 do 2 watch 3 listen to 4 play 5 use 6 read

2
1 play 2 read 3 watched 4 does 5 listen to 6 listen to
7 watch 8 use

3
1 read 2 listen 3 read 4 watch 5 watched 6 watch
7 uses 8 listens to 9 plays 10 do

4
1 like; love 2 like; going 3 like; shopping 4 doing; hate
5 listening to; loves 6 travelling; hate

5
1 watching 2 watching 3 reading 4 cooking 5 making
6 making 7 playing 8 reading 9 listening to 10 doing
11 cleaning 12 doing

6
1 Emily loves drawing pictures. Oliver doesn't like/enjoy drawing
pictures.
2 Emily loves watching TV. Oliver doesn't like/enjoy watching TV.
3 Emily doesn't like/enjoy listening to music. Oliver loves listening
to music.
4 Emily likes/enjoys playing video games. Oliver hates playing
video games.
5 Emily hates swimming. Oliver loves swimming.
6 Emily loves dancing. Oliver likes/enjoys dancing.

9C

1
1 write 2 pass 3 make 4 do 5 take 6 remember
7 use 8 fail

2
1 c 2 d 3 e 4 g 5 a 6 h 7 f 8 b

3
1 do 2 did 3 didn't 4 did 5 haven't 6 were 7 did
8 is

4
1 f 2 b 3 d 4 e 5 c 6 a

5

1 Why do you like studying English?
2 Why is Carlos in the library?
3 Why haven't you got a pen?
4 Why didn't you study last night?
5 Why are you sad?
6 Why did you take a Japanese course?
7 Why didn't John pass the exam?
8 Why has Marta got three dictionaries.

9D

1

1 d 2 h 3 a 4 i 5 g 6 b 7 f 8 c 9 e

2

1 Let's do something   2 Good idea   3 Shall we go
4 What shall we watch   5 I saw that last week
6 When shall we go

7 That's a great idea   8 Where shall we go
9 I don't really like Mexican food   10 Shall we go
11 When shall we go   12 Let's go

Listening

1

1 four   2 one

2

1 F 2 T 3 T 4 F 5 T 6 F 7 T 8 T 9 F 10 F
11 F 12 T

3

1 Sofia and Marta   2 Onur   3 Onur and Guy   4 Onur
5 Sofia   6 Marta   7 Guy   8 Sofia

Reading

1

c

2

1 b 2 d 3 a

3

1 cycles around the world   2 job   3 slow
4 the north to the south of Italy   5 train   6 loves everything

4

1 4,000 miles
2 his office wasn't near his house; the bus was expensive
3 he didn't do a lot of exercise
4 new places
5 cheap, clean, healthy and quick
6 20 minutes

Writing

1

1 M 2 J 3 J 4 M 5 M 6 J

2

1 why?   2 middle

3

1 I like reading the newspaper because it's interesting.
2 I was late for work because I got up late.
3 I love/like travelling because I like/love seeing new places.
4 I don't like writing in English because it's difficult.
5 I go to the cinema every week because I love watching films.
6 I take the bus to work because I can't drive.
7 I don't like cleaning the house because it's boring.
8 I didn't go to work yesterday because I cut my hand.

4

1e I don't like living in the city because it's always busy.
2b I like playing football because it's my favourite sport.
3a I never travel by plane because I hate flying.
4f I ride my bike every weekend because I love cycling.
5c I go to the market every week because I love shopping.
6d I go to the theatre once a month because I like watching plays.

5–6

Students' own answers.

UNIT 10

10A

1

1 f 2 g 3 j 4 i 5 b 6 c 7 e 8 d 9 a 10 h

2

1 changed   2 joined   3 built   4 spend   5 had   6 made
7 try   8 sold   9 moved   10 started

3

1 spend   2 change   3 try   4 moved   5 joined   6 made

4

1 b 2 a 3 b 4 b 5 b 6 a 7 b 8 b

5

1 They **would like** to have children in the future.
2 Jan would love **to start** a clothes company.
3 A: Would you like to go to his party?
   B: No, I **wouldn't**.
4 ✓
5 What **would** you like to watch at the cinema tonight?
6 I love my house, so I **wouldn't** like to move.
7 ✓
8 James would like **to join** the gym.

6

1 Where would you like to go … ?
2 Would you like to watch … ?
3 What would Sara like to study … ?
4 What would you like to do in the future?
5 What languages would you like to speak?
6 Would you like to join a gym?

10B

1

1 sing   2 salad   3 sandwiches   4 drinks   5 snacks
6 dessert   7 dance   8 talk   9 listen   10 fruit   11 play

2

1 d 2 b 3 e 4 a 5 c

3

1 I'm going to visit my parents.
2 Lucia is going to come to my house.
3 We are going to watch a film.
4 They are not going to play football.
5 The party is going to be at a restaurant.
6 She is going to arrive at 8 o'clock.
7 I'm going to move to a new house.
8 Edward isn't going to go to school.

4

1 **I'm** going to study French next year.
2 My brother's going **to** change jobs next month.
3 Charlotte and Leonie **are** going to visit the museum.
4 I'm not going **to do** anything on Saturday!
5 They aren't going **to** take the train to Paris.
6 We **aren't** going to play the game.
7 **I'm going** to have dinner with Martin tomorrow.
8 Jenny **is** going to have a baby next year.

5

1 'm/am going to see
2 aren't/are not going to go
3 's/is going to open
4 are going to sell
5 's/is going to change
6 isn't/is not going to move
7 're/are going to play
8 'm/am not going to dance

10c

1

1 January 2 February 3 March 4 April 5 May 6 June
7 July 8 August 9 September 10 October 11 November
12 December

2

1 summer 2 fortnight 3 for 4 in 5 with 6 on 7 th
8 winter 9 for 10 st

3

1 Are you; I'm not 2 Are we; we are 3 to watch; We're
4 Is; isn't 5 are; are 6 are; I'm

4

1 Are you going to study history at university next year?
2 Are you going to move to another city next year?
3 Is Duncan going to play football tomorrow?
4 Are Emma and George going to visit us this weekend?
5 Are we going to be late for class?
6 Are they going to learn Spanish?
7 Is Alex going to make dinner tonight?
8 Are you going to take the train to London?

5

a we're not b we're not c they are d she is e he isn't
f I'm not g they are h I am

6

1 f 2 h 3 e 4 g 5 b 6 c 7 d 8 a

10d

1

1 c 2 a 3 d 4 b

2

1 e 2 c 3 d 4 b 5 f 6 a

Listening

1

Jack: art teacher
Sabrina: police officer

2

c 1 f 2 e 3 b 4 a 5 d 6

3

1 J 2 S/J 3 J 4 S 5 S/J 6 S

4

1 a 2 b 3 b 4 b 5 b 6 b

Reading

1

a clothes company

2

a 2 b 3 c 1

3

1 F (Amy Hughes has got two clothes shops.)
2 T
3 F (Now she only sells clothes for children.)
4 F (In the future, she'd like to make shoes.)
5 T
6 F (She'd like to join a gym and do more exercise.)

4

1 In 2014.
2 She was very busy and didn't spend time with her family and friends.
3 Next year.
4 In London.
5 Lots of different places.
6 A big house by the sea.

Writing

1

Sophie; Josie

2

1 Marco 2 Sophie 3 Josie 4 Elif

3

1 They 2 them 3 them

4

1 it 2 They 3 us 4 She 5 him 6 them

5

1 In the summer holidays, I'm going to go to Italy with my friend. **We** are going to take the boat.
2 I can't speak Spanish, but I'm going to study **it** next year.
3 Dan loves music, but **he** can't sing!
4 My parents live in New York. I'm going to visit **them** next year.
5 Jane and I lived together for two years. **We** had a flat in the centre of Madrid.
6 Sam made pizza last night. **It** was great!

6

1 It 2 They 3 them 4 She 5 her 6 we

7–8
Students' own answers.